14/22

agamemnon

a collection of essays edited by
david stuttard and tamsin shasha

aod publications • brighton

published by
aod publications

© **aod** 2002

actors of dionysus,
44-46 old steine, brighton, uk bn1 1nh

t +0044 1273 320 396
f +0044 1273 220 025
e info@actorsofdionysus.com
www.actorsofdionysus.com

aod publications

essays on agamemnon

Essays on Agamemnon is published in association with **aod** (Actors of Dionysus), the UK's leading theatre company dedicated to classical Greek drama.

Founded in 1993 by David Stuttard and Tamsin Shasha, **aod** eschews a traditional "archaeological" approach, seeking to bring the plays vividly alive for a modern generation and working with practitioners such as Thea Barnes from *Phoenix Dance* and Marcello Magni from *Theatre de Complicité.*

aod tours regularly throughout the British Isles and, for its tenth anniversary, has been invited to perform in Greece, Turkey and Croatia.

In addition to productions and publications, **aod** runs a strong educational programme, including workshops and summer schools. Talks are given before certain performances by leading scholars, many of whom have contributed to this collection of essays.

aod has broadcast on BBC Radio 3, and its audiobook of *Medea* was released worldwide by Penguin in 1997. *The Independent* described Tamsin Shasha's performance in the central role as "chillingly convincing", while *The Financial Times* said that the performances "make it clear why the Greeks were so excited about this play more than a millennium ago".

aod's stage performances have been described by *The Guardian* as "direct and accessible", by *The Irish Times* as "perfectly pitched" and by *The Yorkshire Evening Press* as "seriously sexy", while *The Times* wrote that "they perform these ancient stories with such conviction that they bring tears to the eyes and make the hair at the nape of the neck bristle. Let nothing stop you from seeing them!"

David Stuttard studied classics at St. Andrews University and directs regularly for **aod**. He has translated twelve plays for production and adapted five. His own play, *Blow Your Mind, Aristophanes!*, was staged in association with Channel 4 and the British Film Institute, and his translation of *Agamemnon*, part-supported by The Arts Council of England, has been adopted as a set text by The Open University for their course, *Europe: Culture and Identities in a Contested Continent*.

Tamsin Shasha took a degree at Newcastle before training as an actor at The Oxford School of Drama. For **aod**, she has played a number of tragic heroines on stage, video and audiobook. In addition to her acting roles, she has been movement director on several productions, and in 2002 directed three tragedies in David Stuttard's adaptation at Epidavros in Greece.

Foreword

Written in 458 BCE, *Agamemnon* is the first play in the *Oresteian Trilogy*, Aeschylus' epic dramatic exploration of the cycle of killing and revenge within the House of Atreus.

Its scope is huge, its structure complex. Swept forward by the action of the play, we are at the same time dragged back through the generations towards the murky roots of family conflict in the sacrifice of Agamemnon's daughter, Iphigenia, and the cannibal feast of his father Atreus.

To his layers of temporal narrative, Aeschylus adds a further dimension, for his is a world populated not only by men and women but by gods and spirits, ghosts and avenging demons, a world of omens and of visions, where the fate of every living creature is inexorably and perilously intertwined.

Deliberately archaic in its style, *Agamemnon* makes brilliant use of the chorus, using them now as narrators, weaving bold and dazzling images, now as actors in the drama.

Aeschylus populates his world with beautifully rounded and memorable characters: from the self-effacing Watchman who begins the play to the Herald, strutting, garrulous; to the tragic, brave Cassandra; and Agamemnon, terrifying in his ignorance and self-delusion.

But the crowning glory of the play is Clytemnestra, Agamemnon's wife, manipulative, awesome, always in control, the spider at the centre of a web of treachery.

I translated *Agamemnon* first in 1999 for performance by Actors of Dionysus. The translation has subsequently been adopted by the Open University for their course, AA300 – Europe: Culture and Identities in a Contested Continent, to be introduced in 2003. 2003 is also **aod**'s tenth anniversary year, and to mark it the company will stage a new production of the play.

It was to coincide with this that we asked some of the leading classicists in the British Isles to contribute to this collection of essays.

Tamsin and I are grateful to all those who responded for their commitment and enthusiasm, to Zara Plessard in the **aod** office and to John and Stan at Hamilton Printing, Hull for their patience, help and advice - and to Mark Katz and EJ Birtwell for their support, understanding and good-humour.

David Stuttard
Brighton, August 2002

Contents

The contributors

Sir Kenneth Dover is Chancellor of the University of St. Andrews

Edith Hall is Levenhulme Professor of Greek Cultural History at the University of Durham

Alex Garvie is Professor of Greek at the University of Glasgow

Carmel McCallum Barry lectures in Classics at University College, Cork

Jasper Griffin is Public Orator for Oxford University and Professor of Classical Literature at Balliol College

Dr. Ruth Hazel is an associate lecturer in Classics at The Open University

David Raeburn, formerly lectured at New College, Oxford, and regularly directs Greek tragedies at Cambridge and Bradfield

Dr. Lorna Hardwick is senior lecturer in Classics at the Open University

agamemnon

There was a man once
reared a lion-cub in the palace.
All unweaned
it loved to suckle,
still so tame, so tender in its infancy.
The children loved it and the old men pampered it,
and in their arms they cradled it
just like a new-born child,
bright-eyed and purring,
feeding from their outstretched hands.

But gradually it grew
and it revealed its innate character.
It showed its gratitude
to those who'd nurtured it,
and of its own will it
prepared a feast, insatiate,
a butchery, a shambles and
the house dripped viscous as an abattoir,
that no-one might outleap the horror or
escape the mutilation,
the bloody devastation that engulfed it.
A priest of sacrifice,
an agent of obsession,
it had been reared by God's will in the family,
to cleanse the household.

Klytaimestra Triumphant

Sir Kenneth Dover

When the Greeks had finally demolished Troy, their commanders, each with his own contingent, went back to their home cities in mainland Greece. But Agamemnon, their supreme commander in the war, was going home to his death, for so it was plotted by his wife Klytaimestra and his cousin Aigisthos, now her lover. Agamemnon's murder is the central point of Aeschylus's play.

The story was much older than the play, as we know from its depiction in vase-painting, citations from early lyric poetry, and above all from a number of detailed allusions in the *Odyssey*. In one of those allusions we are told that Aigisthos posted a lookout to warn him in good time of Agamemnon's arrival. Now, at the beginning of the play, we are presented with a man who has been watching a year long for the sight of a distant beacon which will bring the message, "Troy has fallen". But this man is not the man we have met in the Homeric story; he has been posted not by Aigisthos (of whom he says nothing), but by Klytaimestra, and it is to her, whom he calls "the one who has a man's brain in a woman's body", that he cries out the good news conveyed by the beacon. The man himself is overjoyed, because he is a devoted servant of Agamemnon; and yet he ends his monologue with a disturbing reservation, expressed only by innuendo: "This house, this building, if it could but speak, would say it all most clearly." The legend being so long established and so well known, we, the audience, do not need to be told that Klytaimestra has a "man's brain"; she is the most famous of female killers, and killing is a man's business – killing, that is, by a weapon in one's hand, for a queen can order an execution, and in the generation before Aeschylus, according to a narrative given by Herodotus, a queen of Cyrene revenged herself on the rebellious people of Barke by having the principal rebels impaled around the city walls and their wives' breasts cut off and used as a frieze. Plainly, in a monarchical state such as the myths of the heroic age presuppose the queen can rule in the absence of the king. Klytaimestra has ruled in the absence of Agamemnon, but in the great age of Athenian tragedy, the fifth century BCE, monarchies were few and marginal in the Greek world. The Athens of Aeschylus was a *demokratia* in which women were not permitted to hold secular office or to take decisions affecting the adult male citizens. The popular notion was that women are by nature timorous, inconstant, capricious, unreliable. That is why comedies (such as *Lysistrata*) in which women get together and organise themselves efficiently would have appealed to an Athenian male audience as essentially humorous fantasy, much as when animals, birds or fishes organise themselves politically. It is also why the great enduring myths on which the tragic poets so often drew focus on exceptional women: not only Klytaimestra, but Elektra, Antigone, Phaidra,

Prokne, Eriphyle. Homicide and self-sacrifice, precisely because they are unusual and unexpected, make a story; washing-up does not.

The Chorus in *Agamemnon* echo the Watchman's phrase, "a man's brain in a woman's body"; when Klytaimestra has offered them the full story of the transmission of the news by the beacon-chain, they praise her by saying "your words were like a man's". At that point, they have little choice; their first reaction to her announcement had been to attribute her assurance to a "dream" or a "rumour", and she slaps that down sharply, saying "Don't speak to me as if I were a child!" Yet they cannot abstain for long from the characteristic Greek devaluation of women: just before the arrival of the Herald they contemplate the possibility that the news is false: "What can you expect when a woman's in control? ... A woman's gossip spreads like wildfire..."

The arrival of the Herald settles the issue; the Queen was right after all, the message of the beacons was true. In the presence of the Herald, and even more strikingly in the presence of Agamemnon himself, when he has returned, she is the very model of a submissive wife to whom her husband's well-being is all the world, sleepless and tearful throughout his long absence, impelled by rumours of his death to attempt suicide. All that she says is designed to excite pity and express love, though both the excitation and the expression are warped by rhetoric.

After she has killed her husband, her proud, defiant entry and her frankly brutal speech to the Chorus transport us unto another world, the epic battlefield, of which the "Battle at the Ships" in Book 13 of the *Iliad* provides the most memorable example. The combatant prays for success before he strikes; the lethal wound suffered by the victim is specified in gruesome detail; the victor stands over his dying opponent (Menelaus actually plants his foot on Peisander's chest); the victor utters a cry of triumph, sometimes charged with mockery and grim humour. Klytaimestra's prayer for victory ("Zeus, Zeus ... now fulfil my prayers!") was uttered as the king walked into the palace. Now she declares that the murder was vengeance that had been long planned. "I stand", she says, "where I struck him". Two blows laid him low, and a third ended his life; dying, he coughed a spray of blood over his killer, at which, she says, she rejoiced as the growing corn does "when Zeus sends down his rain". Nowhere else in the play is the conventional contrast between male and female so vividly expressed as when Klytaimestra answers the Chorus's question, "How can you boast that you've killed your own husband?" by saying simply, "You question me as if I were some brainless *woman*!"

An Athenian prosecuted for homicide in a lawcourt during Aeschylus's lifetime – or, indeed, at any other time in the history of the Athenian democracy – could not have expected to win the favour of a jury if he presented his actions in such terms. The sentiment that it is uncivilized to exult *openly* over the death of an enemy, a sentiment impressed by Odysseus on his old nurse Eurykleia when the sight of the slaughtered suitors elicits a cry of joy from her, was widely disseminated.

It is also extremely unlikely that an Athenian wife charged on good evidence with the murder of her husband could have offered any excuse or justification which might in any way have preserved her moral and social standing in the eyes and memory of the community. That does not inhibit Klytaimestra's insistence that her killing of Agamemnon was vengeance, the infliction of a *just* punishment. The crime that demanded punishment was his sacrifice, at the bidding of Kalchas, the chief seer, of his – and her – daughter Iphigeneia, whom she calls "my baby I loved more than anything" and "our child, the child I bore him".

Human sacrifice, though a feature of some myths, was not practised in the Greek world in the time of Aeschylus. Not, at any rate, in a form to which we would readily apply the term, or to which the Greeks themselves applied worlds equivalent to "sacrifice"; nevertheless a genre of infanticide was indeed practised. That was the "exposure" of a newborn child, whose death would be certain unless s/he were taken up by someone who wanted a baby – for instance, a couple grieving for a stillborn baby of their own. It is hardly necessary to ask what happened if parents disagreed on whether a newborn child should be exposed, for we know enough about Greek society to assure us that it is men who won such arguments, and in any case acknowledgement by the father was a necessary condition of legitimacy. It is, however, worthwhile to ask what happened when a decision to expose a baby had been taken by the father against the mother's will. If we ask for hard evidence, we ask in vain, but I find speculation irresistible, and what makes it so is the possibility that Klytaimestra's relentless pursuit of revenge for Iphigeneia's death is a reflex of an issue not unknown to the audience.

The injection of contemporary conflicts into the tragic poets' handling of myth is on occasion demonstrable, the best-known relevant text being Medea's complaint about the unfortunate lot of women, a complaint which ends with the memorable declaration, "I would rather stand three times in line of battle than give birth once". We sometimes hear the passage dismissed on the grounds that Medea is a barbarian murderess whose sentiments would have repelled a decent Athenian matron, but such an interpretation ignores the fact that in the lost *Tereus* of Sophocles the same depressing view of women in Greek society is taken by Prokne, who is an Athenian princess (and, like Medea, murders her son to take revenge on her atrocious husband).

Sixteen years before Aeschylus's play Pindar, in his 11th Pythian victory-ode, poses a rhetorical question: *why* did Klytaimestra kill Agamemnon and Kassandra? He puts forward two alternative reasons, and leaves us to choose: was she irreconcilably angered by the sacrifice of Iphigeneia, or was she seduced by Aigisthos? Seduction by Aigisthos was the answer given long before Homer, who never mentions the sacrifice of Iphigeneia. It is a motive comparatively inconspicuous in Aeschylus, whose Aigisthos is vilified by the Chorus as "Coward!" and "Woman!". He had a strong motive of his own for revenge, which he expounds when he appears at the end of the play, but he does not cut a convincing figure as a man likely to take the initiative in seducing so formidable a woman. Anger over Iphigeneia, on the other hand, is brought into great prominence as her motive by the attention given to it in the first chorus of the play.

One of the most striking features of that chorus is the fact that it nowhere says that Artemis demanded the sacrifice of Iphigeneia; it says rather that Kalchas the seer *said* that she did, and that Agamemnon "did not blame Kalchas for his prophecies"; and at the climax of the grisly story, that "Kalchas' visions come to pass". From what Klytaimestra says of the reason for the sacrifice, a brief, dismissive allusion, we would hardly know that prophecy and the interpretation of omens came into it at all. That would be by no means alien to tragedy, since a tragic character (like a

7

real person) can brush aside a prophecy or interpretation of an omen, even an oracle (as Jocasta does in *Oedipus Rex*), if it is unwelcome.

We have come to the point at which *justice* is the issue. Klytaimestra demands: if you threaten me with exile because I have killed my husband, why did you not impose exile on my husband because he killed our daughter? Cool discussion, let alone agreement, on such a question is hardly to be expected. And yet, for a moment, the contestants do agree, for the Chorus says, "You've brought the demon to the daylight ..., a plague on the household", and Klytaimestra responds, "You see it now for what it is ..., the demon which has gorged itself three times upon this family". The Greek word, *daimon*, is the ancestor of our "demon", but much wider in meaning, for it may mean "god", and it may be the "fate" of an individual, beneficent or malign. Having seen and heard Kassandra in the throes of her dreadful visions, we know that there is indeed a curse hanging over the family, and the *daimon* here is the supernatural entity brought into being when a curse is accepted by Zeus (a curse is, after all, a species of prayer) and activated as circumstances permit. But Klytaimestra goes a stage further in suggesting that the inherited curse has actually taken on human form, *her* form, so that the adversary of the Chorus, who is indeed the murderer of Agamemnon, is no more than a simulacrum. The concept is not unique, for in one of the myths of the Trojan War a simulacrum of Helen was present in Troy while the real Helen stayed in Egypt. The point of that story was to absolve Helen of adultery; absolution from murder is a different matter, and the Chorus reject the idea emphatically: "What? Are you guiltless of his murder? ... How could it be?" And yet, immediately, they back-track by saying "Perhaps a demon of revenge ... *might* come as an accomplice".

Such judicious words ring strangely in a scene permeated by emotion incompatible with a cool allocation of responsibility, but they conform to that banal, helpless admission, "The truth is hard to judge", which comes just before the entry of Aigisthos and his redirection of the issue to justice and revenge (he says he can "die content" now that he has seen the son of the man who had so cruelly wronged *his* family laid low in death). "The truth is hard to judge" might be said at many points in the story. It could never be known for sure whether Kalchas was right in believing that the goddess Artemis demanded the sacrifice of the king's daughter, or whether the adverse winds were a manifestation of her anger in the first place, or whether the sacrifice actually made them stop (spells of bad weather do, after all, stop eventually, as Herodotus recognised when he spoke of the calming of a storm by ritual during the Persian invasion of Greece). Should Agamemnon have refused to comply with Kalchas's recommendation? And anyway, *could* he have done so? Was the predicament in which he found himself divinely constructed for the purpose of fulfilling the curse which had been

9

uttered against his father? (How does one know when a curse has been, so to speak, "registered" by the gods for eventual fulfilment?) And how could Klytaimestra know, how can the audience know, whether she was the embodiment of a curse, and thus the instrument of a being other than herself, or an autonomous, responsible human? The obstinate fact that all such questions defy attempts to answer them by rational demonstration, and actually receive answers only in accordance with the parti-pris of the individual who speaks – as when Priam in the third book of the *Iliad* consoles Helen by saying "I don't blame you <sc. for the war>; it's the *gods* that I blame" – is one of the most productive sources of tragic fiction.

If we know the rest of the story, the return of Orestes and his killing of his mother and Aigisthos in revenge for Agamemnon – and the use of the story in poetry and art, together with Kassandra's unambiguous prophecy, has planted it firmly in our minds – we may well consider that Aeschylus wishes us to regard Klytaimestra, after the entry of Aigisthos and the threat of imminent killing if the Chorus are attacked by his bodyguard, as horribly aware that there is more blood to be shed, hers in particular. "No! No!" she cries to her lover, "There's been enough suffering, so no more blood." She has come now to see a long chain of retaliations stretching into the future, and she does not like what she sees. She is no longer the triumphant figure who stood over the corpse of Agamemnon.

Eating Children is Bad for You: The Offspring of the Past in Aeschylus' *Agamemnon*

Edith Hall

> Our deeds are like children that are
> born to us; they live and act apart
> from our will; nay, children may be
> strangled, but deeds never; they
> have an indestructible life, both in
> and out of our consciousness.
>
> (George Eliot)

The Infancy of Humankind

In one of the most extraordinary ghost scenes in world literature, the clairvoyant Cassandra of *Agamemnon* sees the spectres of the little children served up at the Thyestean feast, diminutive ghosts who died in and haunt the house forming the scenic background to the tragedy. "Do you see those young creatures", she demands of the chorus, "beside the house, like figures in dreams? They are the children slaughtered by their own kindred; their hands are full of the meat of their own flesh; they are clear to me, holding their vitals and entrails, which their father tasted" (1217-22). As if to emphasise her isolation, Aeschylus has designed the scene so that only Cassandra can see these very special spirits of the untimely dead - pitiful, butchered, roasted, and disembowelled. The chorus and the audience, in contrast, must rely upon their imaginations.

Inter-reacting with Cassandra's vision of the ghostly, cannibalised sons of Thyestes, numerous metaphorical and symbolic children haunt the imagery and figures of speech characterising the tragedy as a whole. The chorus complain about growing old; they are as weak and ineffectual as children (75, 81). At Troy, says Clytemnestra, children are being thrown onto the corpses of the very men who begot them (327-8). Temptation, state the chorus, is a domineering child who incites a man to arrogant behaviour (385-6); such an arrogant man is, in his delusion, like a child who chases a bird (394). Clytemnestra complains about being addressed as if she were a child of no understanding (277); childishness is equated with a lack of sense or comprehension (479). When the chorus can finally understand unambiguously something that Cassandra says (i.e., that she is about to die), they reply that "even a newborn infant" could understand her words (1163). Aegisthus also contributes to the repertoire of infancy images: he describes how he was sent into exile by Atreus when he was still only in swaddling-bands (1606).

It is not easy to understand this pervasive equation of imperfect powers of comprehension with those of children in isolation from the other plays in the *Oresteia*. In the course of the tragedies Aeschylus uses the analogy of the life of a human being to symbolise the progress of humankind as a whole from barbarism to civilisation. In terms of the advance of civilisation, the people in *Agamemnon* still remain in their infancy; in *Libation-Bearers* Orestes is at the point of leaving adolescence; by the stage of human development portrayed in *Eumenides*, the Argive prince, who now represents a new level of social evolution, has himself become an adult and can be tried as a morally competent and autonomous agent in a civil court. The course of a human life - from birth through babyhood, infancy, childhood and adolescence to adulthood - is thus used as a paradigm of the progress of Greek society from the moral toy box of simple, reciprocal blood-feuds to the complexities of "grown-up", publicly administered justice.

The Offspring of the Past

From the ancient Greeks of Aeschylus' time the legacy of past deeds were conceptualised more concretely, more externally, and more physically than it is in our modern notions of internal guilt which torments the malefactor. Murderers (and there was no crime more serious than murder within the family, outlawed by an ancient and grave taboo) were tormented not so much by their own consciences as by the Erinyes, or vengeance-spirits, of the murdered victim. The Erinyes could only be appeased by the blood of the murderer, or vicariously by the blood of his or her children. When this blood was spilt on the ground, they drank it voraciously from their subterranean home beneath it.

The Erinyes are not pleasant. Like most monstrous collectives in Greek myth, they are female. Gruesome descriptions of them are available in the last play of the trilogy, *Eumenides*: they are wingless, black, bloodsucking, polluting, snort awful blasts from their nostrils, ooze filthy mucus from their eyes, and wear disgusting clothes. Apollo says that they belong in a torture chamber, "where men are beheaded, have their eyes gouged out, are castrated, mutilated, are stoned to death, and, impaled beneath the spine, moan long and piteously" (186-90). In this last play of the trilogy the Erinyes who act on behalf of the dead Clytemnestra actually appear to the audience, in the form of the chorus; they have to be appeased by Athena when she takes away their right to avenge murder, replacing them jurisprudentially with the gods' new invention - a state-administered homicide court. Aeschylus' Erinyes were so frightening in appearance that the ancient *Life of Aeschylus* claimed that pregnant women in the original audience actually suffered spontaneous miscarriages. This biographical anecdote is probably not true. But the emergence of the story in later antiquity reveals another kind of truth: it preserves an authentic response to the emphasis in the *Oresteia* on dead infants and on the process of mammalian reproduction.

The "offspring of the past", whose deaths eventually all operate as sacrifices to appease the Erinyes, form the central Argive triangle of

Agamemnon: Agamemnon,   his   wife
Clytemnestra, and his cousin (and her lover)
Aegisthus. None of them can eradicate past
deeds: their actions in the play are direct results
of the past actions (especially infanticide)
committed by themselves, their parents, or in
Clytemnestra's   case   her   husband.
Agamemnon's father had murdered his brother
Thyestes' children, which Aegisthus cannot
forgive, since they were his own brothers.
Thyestes had seduced his brother's wife;
Agamemnon had slaughtered his own daughter
Iphigenia. The deaths of both Thyestes' children
and of the young Iphigenia have left a horrific
legacy of Erinyes thirsting for blood. Aeschylus,
in composing a tragedy about the death of
Agamemnon, chose a particular moment, a
period of hours between dawn and dusk, in which
he is murdered. But in the compass of that single
day Aeschylus conveys to his audience a
panoramic transhistorical vision, delving into the
past through the successive crimes in the family
descending from Atreus, and also envisioning its
equally miserable future: Cassandra predicts
explicitly the deaths of "another woman" and
"another man" (1317-18). The architecture of the
tragedy's temporal scheme allows Aeschylus to
unfold the story of the house of Atreus across
three blighted generations.   The three central
characters have little sense of the large wheels in
which they are but small cogs. But by careful use
of the chorus, of the seer Cassandra, and of the
imagery of human and animal reproduction,
Aeschylus allows his audience a much more

comprehensive and transhistorical grasp of the endlessly self-replicating revenge murders blighting Argos.

Eating Children

Eating children is not just bad for the children and the consumer's digestion. In ancient Greek myth it is bad for the entire extended family, affecting them down the generations. Kin-killing was one of the most serious offences Greek ethics could imagine. But compounding it with the eating of human flesh outraged every religious sensibility. The two fathers of Agamemnon and Aegisthus had between them contrived to do both at the same time: they had compounded kin-killing with cannibalism. Cannibalism (which in this instance, since Thyestes was unaware of what he was eating, would more correctly be termed "anthropophagy"), was presented in even the earliest Greek literature as a sign of the utmost barbarism: Achilles imagines devouring part of Hector raw in the *Iliad* (22.346-8), but even in his wildest fits of anger stops short of such an atrocity. Human flesh-eating in Greek thought is only practised by such cultural outlaws as the Cyclopes of the *Odyssey*, and remote savages located by ethnographers beyond the margins of civilisation. The eating of humans by humans is explicitly proscribed in Hesiod (*Works and Days* 276-80), for consuming members of your own species is regarded as the way of beasts. If humans are to preserve that important boundary between themselves and animals, they must absolutely abjure the consumption of human flesh.

Agamemnon is concerned with an incident but a generation ago when human flesh - indeed human *infant* flesh - was undeniably eaten. This incident is one of the most repellent episodes in Greek myth; it is portrayed in the tragedy as an outrage which threatened to annihilate all distinctions between humanity and bestiality. It was planned by Agamemnon's father Atreus as a personal assault on his brother, Thyestes, who also happened to be Aegisthus' father. Aegisthus escaped ending up in a saucepan with his brothers, an escape he seems to explain by saying that he had at the time been just a tiny baby, not yet out of swaddling clothes (1606). The two leading men in the tragedy, Agamemnon and Aegisthus, are thus bound together not only by their shared woman, Clytemnestra, but by the horrible knowledge of what had happened on that unspeakable day when the father of one had served up to the father of the other his very own children's flesh.

Aeschylus' poetry in *Agamemnon* is not gentle on its audience's sensibilities. It contains some of the bloodiest language and imagery in Greek tragedy. Even though something has happened to shorten or distort the transmission of the Greek text of Aegisthus' description of the Thyestean feast, and even though it does not approach the nauseating extension and detail of the equivalent passage in Seneca (the messenger speech of

Thyestes), it certainly conveys the physical reality of the occasion when, just inside the walls the audience can see, the tiny bodies were literally "butchered", devoured, and regurgitated. In Aegisthus' embittered account, Atreus could not forgive Thyestes for trying to appropriate his throne, and so he summoned him to a festival. But first he killed his nephews, broke off their fingers and toes so as to disguise the nature of the flesh, and then served them up to his brother. When Thyestes realised what he had eaten, "he let forth a great cry, reeled back, vomited forth the slaughtered flesh", and cursed the entire family line of Atreus, all his descendants in perpetuity (1590-1602), kicking over the banquet table to underline his curse as he did so.

The Thyestean feast, which happened when Aegisthus and (presumably) Agamemnon were still tiny, is important to the understanding of the tragedy because the murders it enacts, and those to follow in the other plays, are the direct result of the child-killing, the cannibalism, and the curse. This becomes transparently clear in the great Cassandra scene, where her supernatural powers allow her to intuit the entire criminal history of the palace to which she has been brought. What she has to say to the audience, who know her visions are truthful, is absolutely horrific. She says that she has come to a house loathed by heaven, a house which has witnessed the butchering of family members, the slaughter of men, and whose floor is swimming with blood (1090-2). Then she points to the roof of the house, at something unseeable by our eyes or those of the chorus, and screams, "behold those children bewailing their own slaughter and their roasted flesh, eaten by their father" (1095-7). She can hear a chorus of the spirits of dead relatives; another company of the vengeance-spirits of dead kinfolk is haunting the house, chanting a song about the "original crime" (1192). Shortly afterwards Cassandra returns once again to the theme of the ghostly children clutching their own entrails, and delivers the terrible words quoted in the opening paragraph of this essay.

The Imagery of Reproduction

The tragedy extends the imagery of human genesis and reproduction (sometimes called by academics "paedogonic" imagery) to encompass its cosmic and ethical themes. Even the alternation of day and night is conceptualised in terms of childbirth: Clytemnestra, shortly after her entrance, speaks of the morning which is "born from its mother", night (264-5), and subsequently says that the night has "given birth" to the sun (279). The cosmos is conceptualised by the same images of childbirth and reproduction we find elsewhere in the play; but it is particularly appropriate language for a woman whose own role as mother is a crucial issue, and who offers as one ground for her murder of Agamemnon the fact that he had sacrificed her daughter Iphigenia "as if she were an animal", the daughter to whom Clytemnestra recalls giving birth "with the sweetest labour pains" (1415-18). Much earlier in the play mammalian gestation has been central to the chorus' sung account of the omen which precipitated the sacrifice of Iphigenia: two eagles had appeared near the palace, and had devoured a pregnant hare, including her unborn brood (114-120). This disgusting picture of two birds devouring another creature's foetuses, while obviously relevant to the theme of infant-flesh-eating, also introduces the god Artemis. It is she who is angered, as the deity responsible for lion cubs and suckling young (140-5), and who demands the sacrifice of *human* young before the Greeks can leave for Troy.

One of the most illuminating animal images occurs in the chorus' actual description of the sacrifice of Iphigenia. The play throughout implies that Agamemnon has inherited his infanticidal tendencies from his father Atreus, who blurred that vital distinction between animals and beasts by forcing his brother into anthropophagy. Agamemnon similarly blurs this distinction, by offering a human sacrifice instead of an animal one. Greek literature universally presents human sacrifice as an abomination, practised only by Carthaginians and other barbarians on the margins of the civilised world. Yet Agamemnon chose to have his daughter Iphigenia sacrificed "like a kid" (231-8); she has a bit in her mouth to gag her, like a young animal, and is substituted for the fawn or other wild sacrificial beast which would have been the customary offering to Artemis.

Thus the omen of the eagles and the pregnant hare thematically prefigures the death of Iphigenia. It also makes concrete the overarching theme of the child-destroying family curse, a curse which affects children born to the household even before their birth. Agamemnon was once the innocent little child of Atreus; the stage building representing Atreus' physical house, a psychoanalytical critic might suggest, becomes itself an enormous, toxic, lethal womb. It disgorges the bloodied corpse of Agamemnon, killed like a defenceless baby in the amniotic fluid of his homecoming bath; he is dragged alongside Cassandra, stillborn or aborted in a sinister parody of a multiple birth, through the vulva-like doors of the palace into the harsh daylight of Argos. In the polysemic world of Aeschylean poetry it is not too outrageous to see the killing of Agamemnon and Cassandra, enclosed within the stage doors, as prefigured by the omen where the eagles killed the unborn children of the hare, still embryos in their mother's womb.

Yet the most important dimension of the child-producing imagery, the most informative use of the Greek terminology of begetting, conception, and engendering, is the way it formulates the ethical ideas which lie at the heart of the play's conception of human action. Half-way through the play the chorus await the return of their king, and try to sort out their thoughts about the Argive crisis. "It is", they assert trenchantly, "the evil deed which thereafter begets more evil deeds, in breed like itself" (758-60). In *Agamemnon* the king's downfall is caused specifically by the working out of the curse, sworn by Thyestes at the Thyestean feast, against the offspring of Atreus. The chorus believe that it is not prosperity itself which causes the destruction of a household (a traditional and widespread view), but a single iniquitous deed. The evil deed begets more evil deeds, in breed like itself (758-60). The criminal act spawns more criminal acts. The chorus' metaphorical family of parent crimes and child crimes then almost imperceptibly mutates into the physical reality of a human family: the doer of the evil deed begets further doers of evil deeds. With another slide between concrete and metaphorical families the doer then becomes the deed again: an act of hubris in the past, the chorus continue, "begets" an act of hubris in the present; the "children" of hubris curse the household, but are in fact replicas of their hubristic parents (763-6).

There can be no clearer statement that the miseries of a household are the direct result of former crimes in the past. Bad behaviour begets bad behaviour, inherited by each child of a cursed family from its cursed parents. While the idea of an inheritable curse may seem alien and primitive to us, it is worth thinking in terms of modern theories about the adverse effects on children of bad parenting and of poor parental examples. Dysfunctional families do produce more dysfunctional children, who reproduce, when they become parents themselves, the maladjusted behaviours of their own bad parents. Taken from this perspective, the archaic concept of the inheritable curse may not seem so bizarre after all. What is extraordinarily striking is that Clytemnestra, the murderous mother from whose body sprang both the victim Iphigenia and the future avenger Orestes, actually claims that she is the vehicle through which this family curse is working. In her dialogue with the chorus over the corpses she claims that the person they see before them is not Agamemnon's wife: no, she is an avenger (a fine strong word in Greek, *alastor*), wreaking revenge upon Atreus, in offering up his son Agamemnon as a sacrifice to appease the children of Thyestes. She is the spirit of the very curse, she says, delivered by Thyestes at the fatal banquet (1500-4).

The notion of the curse, doomed to work itself out in repeated patterns of behaviour down the generations, is subtly developed in Aeschylus' handling of the traditional material. The two brothers, Atreus and Thyestes, were rivals for the throne of Argos: their two sons, the cousins Agamemnon and Aegisthus, repeat this rivalry over the throne. Thyestes had once, before the fatal feast, been driven into exile by his brother; his baby son Aegisthus was doomed to be similarly exiled, as he tells us on his entrance; and the third-generation male, Orestes, is also in exile throughout the duration of this play. Again, the brothers Atreus and Thyestes had fallen out over a woman:Thyestes had seduced Atreus' wife Aerope, indeed eventually married her. Atreus and Thyestes' two sons, Agamemnon and

Aegisthus, follow the identical course in their respective relationships with Clytemnestra. Lastly, the destruction of innocent children has already shown itself to be a recurrent element in this family's dysfunctional activities; Atreus killed his brother's sons; Agamemnon kills his own daughter. It seems that there is no way out of this vicious cycle of recurring violence in the house of Atreus. The past produces offspring in breed like itself.

Natural Law and Jungle Law

But what is the philosophical result of all this astonishing reproductive imagery, imagery which connects dead children across generations through inheritable curses themselves configured linguistically as human infants? Aeschylus' decision to frame the ethical choice as reproductive biological imperative implies that the "system" of reciprocal killing is actually embedded deep within nature. The implication is that humans can only escape the bloody "natural order" with the dawning of a new enlightened age of reason, in which they can demarcate themselves off from animals, and create a higher system of law administered by communities which transcend biological ties. Here the imagery of reproduction becomes inseperable from the proliferation of animal imagery (which has been much more carefully studied by scholars in the past than the repertoire of reproductive terms). The humans at the infantile stage of social development depicted in *Agamemnon* find it almost impossible to conceptualise the universe they inhabit without resorting to analogies with the law of the jungle, or at the very least to the law of the farmyard and of the hunt. The watchman who delivers the prologue already describes himself as a "hound", who must place the "ox" of silence on his tongue (3, 36). The Argive battle-cry was like the scream of eagles who have lost their babies, and wheel in lonely bereavement over their empty nest (48-54); the Argives were like a ravening lion who drank the blood of Troy (824-8); we are reminded that they sprang from the insides of the wooden horse; like newborn foals springing from the mare's womb, they were "the brood of the horse" (824-8). Clytemnestra complains that buzzing mosquitoes awoke her from her dreams (891-4); but she herself strikes one speaker or another as a hound, a snake, a lioness (1258-9), a croaking raven (1473), and twice as a spider in whose web Agamemnon died (1115, 1492). At the end of the play the chorus insultingly refer to her and Aegisthus as a hen and a cock (1671). Agamemnon comes to be equated with a bull, a hound, and a lion (1125-6). Cassandra is variously likened to a swallow (1050), a newly captured wild animal (1063), a hound (1093), a nightingale (1141-2), a sacrificial ox (1298), and a swan (1445-6), who saves its last song for the moment of its death. The nightingale is a particularly appropriate example, for the mythical precursor of the nightingale was an Athenian princess called Procne who slaughtered her own son Itys, and vengefully served him up in a casserole to Tereus, the murdered child's sadistic rapist of a father. The song of the nightingale was explained by Greek mythology as the infanticidal Procne's unceasing lament for her son.

All these images suggest that in the primitive mythical world of Argos, before the invention of civic justice, humans were social and psychological infants, who still behaved like bloodthirsty animals. The images also imply that they could only think about one another in the images of the bestiary, like insults thrown around a playground, or the animal figures in children's fables and nursery rhymes. It is perhaps in Helen that the connection between the reproductive imagery and the imagery of the jungle is most brilliantly welded. Helen, who arrived in Troy as the beautiful bride of Paris, yet who caused the total destruction of the city, is associated with the potent idea of a lion cub fostered in a household. At first the cub is an adorable, gentle companion, allowed to play with children, and nursed in the arms like a newborn baby; as it grows up, however, it turns fierce and violent, causing terrible carnage and destruction (717-36). It is striking that not only Helen but also Clytemnestra and Agamemnon are connected through imagery with lions. It is tempting to speculate that Aeschylus was perfectly well aware that lions - like his tragic humans - are one of the very few mammalian creatures capable of eating their own children.

Agamemnon: Plot, Tragedy, Imagery, Staging, and Characterisation

Alex Garvie

Aeschylus' *Agamemnon* was originally produced in 458 B.C. as the first part of the *Oresteia* trilogy, which included also *Libation Bearers* (*Grave Gifts* in David Stuttard's translation) and *Eumenides*. Aeschylus wrote other connected trilogies, but this is the only one to survive in its entirety. The original audience saw the three plays on the same day, one after the other. In one sense they resemble the three acts of a modern three-act drama, and one might think that it would be frustrating for a modern audience to see only the first play in isolation. But in fact each play has its own dramatic unity, and a production of any one of them should be a highly rewarding experience. In 458 B.C. Aeschylus was at the height of his powers, and, for many modern readers and audiences, *Agamemnon* is the greatest of his tragedies, and indeed one of the greatest tragedies ever written. The reason may be that it appeals to us in so many ways, in the perfect construction of its plot, in the profundity of its tragic ideas, in the complexity of its poetic imagery, in the consummate theatricality of its staging, in the characterisation of Clytemnestra. Although all of these elements are interrelated, I shall try in this essay to deal with them individually in turn.

I start with plot-construction. The play begins with foreboding. A Watchman on the roof of Agamemnon's palace, waiting for the beacon that will signal the fall of Troy, reveals not only his own physical discomfort, but his fear that something is wrong in the palace, which is at present ruled over by a woman, "the one who has a man's brain in a woman's body". Then he sees the beacon and rejoices, but the rejoicing is short-lived. By the end of the speech he has returned to the idea that the palace contains some dark secret: "this house, this building, if it could but speak, would say it all most clearly". What it is he is too afraid to tell. This movement, from foreboding to joy and then back again to foreboding and still deeper anxiety, is characteristic of the whole of the first part of the play. In its long entrance-song the Chorus, instead of advancing the plot, take us back to the past, to the departure of the Greek expedition to Troy, ten years before, and to Agamemnon's sacrifice of his daughter Iphigeneia to the goddess Artemis at Aulis, in order to secure favourable winds for the voyage. This information about the past could have been narrated to the audience much more briefly in the Watchman's prologue-speech. Instead Aeschylus has chosen to present it to us through the heightened language of lyric poetry, to the accompaniment of music and dancing. The past is not just that which has led to the present; it is already felt to be part of the present action. Technically the play began with the Watchman on the roof, but already we are back at Aulis with Agamemnon ten years earlier, agonising with him as to whether he should sacrifice his daughter.

The song ends, and Clytemnestra enters to announce to the sceptical Chorus the victory of the Greeks. When she describes the chain of beacons that has brought the news from Troy, the Chorus are convinced, and their next song starts as a song of thanksgiving to the gods. But, once more, the joy does not last. As they recall the cost of the war and the suffering and deaths of so many Greeks, "butchered for another's wife (i.e. Helen)", they begin to look ahead to the return home of the king, and turn to wishful thinking, to the hope that the war may not after all be over. The future is too dark for them to face. And so the foreboding continues to build up. The wishful thinking is soon shown to be futile, when a Herald enters to announce the imminent arrival of Agamemnon. Perhaps we were expecting the entrance of the king himself, but Aeschylus is in no hurry to reach that climax. First the Herald must add to the foreboding by recounting the sacrilege committed by the Greeks at Troy, and the divine punishment that has already destroyed most of the fleet in a storm on the homeward voyage; only Agamemnon's ship has reached home safely. He has returned defenceless, and we suspect that the gods have a worse punishment in store for him. In their next song the Chorus take us still further into the past, to Paris's rape of Helen and their flight to Troy. For that crime Paris and the Trojans have now been punished. But what about the crimes of Agamemnon?

When at last Agamemnon enters we already feel that he is doomed, all the more so as he fails to understand the Chorus's hints of the danger from hypocrites waiting for him at home. Clytemnestra greets him, and, although he knows that it is wrong and dangerous, he succumbs to her persuasion to walk over red fabrics or tapestries into the palace. It is clear that we shall never see him again. But before he goes, he has drawn our attention to the figure of Cassandra, his Trojan concubine, who sits beside him in his chariot. We take note of her, but again Aeschylus keeps us waiting to see what role she is going to play. After the Chorus have sung another anxious song, Clytemnestra comes out of the palace to invite Cassandra to enter it to share in the sacrifices. Cassandra makes no reply, and the queen retires defeated. In a remarkable scene the prophetess presents her vision of the king being murdered in his bath, and tells us that she too is going to die. She also takes us back once more into the past, as she presents a vision of the children of Thyestes served up for dinner to their father by his brother Atreus, the father of Agamemnon. Cassandra, as a prophetess, is the only character in the play who can interpret for us both the present and the future in terms of their causal connection with the past, but she is fated never to be believed.

When we hear the offstage death-cries of Agamemnon we can hardly pretend that we are surprised. Suspense, rather than surprise, is the technique regularly exploited by Aeschylus. From the beginning of the play the foreboding has grown stronger and stronger as we have come ever closer to its inevitable fulfilment. But a surprise does come later. Clytemnestra enters to enjoy her triumph over her husband, and to exult in the manner of his death. But even for Clytemnestra the joy will not last. At the end of an angry altercation with the Chorus her mood changes, and she reveals her weariness at the bloodshed in the family, and her hope that she might make a pact with the "demon of revenge", that it might go away and trouble some other family. However, just as some kind of reconciliation seems to be imminent, a new character appears, surprisingly late in the play, the odious Aegisthus, Clytemnestra's paramour, to enjoy his revenge for Atreus' crimes against his father Thyestes. Clytemnestra intervenes to prevent bloodshed between the chorus and Aegisthus and his bodyguard, and the play ends in a kind of deadlock, with the adulterous pair preparing to enjoy their power in the palace. With the mention of the exiled Orestes, son of Agamemnon, Aeschylus prepares us for the second play, in which Orestes will return to take vengeance on his mother and Aegisthus.

How are we to explain Agamemnon's tragedy? From one point of view it all goes back to his sacrifice of Iphigeneia, which the Chorus describe for us in their entrance-song. This is his first crime, and after the murder Clytemnestra makes it clear that revenge for her daughter's death was her principal motive, and she claims to have Justice on her side. But did he have any choice in the matter, and, if so, did he make the wrong choice? Agamemnon's problem is that Zeus himself, the supreme god, has commanded him to lead the expedition against Troy to punish Paris for his rape of Helen. To disobey Zeus would be wrong. But the angry goddess Artemis demands that, in return for favourable winds at Aulis, he must sacrifice his daughter. Agamemnon *does* have a choice, but he is in an impossible situation; whatever he decides will be wrong. When the Chorus say that "he clamped around his throat the leash of certainty" (a metaphor from yoking an animal), the meaning is not that he was somehow fated to kill Iphigeneia, but that the pressure on him to do so was greater than his natural reluctance, or, more simply, that he was forced to make a choice. It is not his fault that he finds himself in this situation. If Paris had not gone off with Helen, Agamemnon would never have had to make his terrible decision. But he *is* responsible for the choice that he makes. All of this may seem to us illogical, but most of us have experienced occasions on which, through no fault of our own, we have been compelled to choose between two courses of action, each of which is likely to lead to trouble. Then, having made his choice, Agamemnon will go on to commit his further crimes, the killing of too many men in the war, the sacrilegious destruction of the Trojan temples. Another factor complicates Agamemnon's tragedy still further. Aeschylus leaves it until the Cassandra scene to present the king as the victim also of the curse pronounced against the family by Thyestes. That the sons are punished for their fathers' sins is an idea that frequently occurs in Greek thought. This is the justification presented by Aegisthus at the end of the play for his part in Agamemnon's murder. He too can claim to have justice on his side. It may seem unfair that Agamemnon, who is responsible for his own crimes, is held responsible also for those of Atreus. But, if one were to make this complaint to Aeschylus, I suspect that he would reply that life *is* unfair, and that we just have to put up with it. In more modern terms it is equally unfair that children should be made to suffer genetic defects inherited from their parents. Agamemnon has inherited not only his father's crimes, but his propensity to commit them.

The whole problem of the relationship between external compulsion and personal responsibility will appear again when we consider Clytemnestra's attempt at justifying her actions. She claims to be the instrument of divine Justice, and we cannot deny that Agamemnon deserves his punishment, just as Paris deserved to be punished by Agamemnon. But Clytemnestra has other, most of them less respectable, motives – her jealousy of Cassandra, her adulterous affair with Aegisthus, and, perhaps above all, her enjoyment of power in Agamemnon's kingdom. From one point of view her killing of her husband was right, from another clearly wrong. In the next play of the trilogy Orestes will take vengeance on his father's behalf by killing Clytemnestra. She too deserves her punishment, but can it ever be right for a son to murder his mother? In addition, then, to engaging his audience's emotional response through his development of mood and atmosphere, Aeschylus appeals also to its intellect. The moral problems of the trilogy are not easily solved, if they can be solved at all.

The moral complexities are balanced by the richness of the poetic language, and by the enormous complexity of interlocking images, especially metaphors. None of Aeschylus' earlier plays comes anywhere near to the *Oresteia* in this respect. Sometimes what is at one point literal turns into metaphor later in the trilogy, or, more often, it is the other way round. Take the theme of light as opposed to darkness. The first, literal, light is seen by the Watchman in the prologue of *Agamemnon*, and Clytemnestra describes for the Chorus the chain of beacons in a speech that is full of words conveying light. Light should be a symbol of victory and hope, but for much of the trilogy it is the metaphorical darkness of fear and foreboding that enshrouds the royal house. Only at the very end of *Eumenides* is the literal light seen at last in a healthy context, as the whole company leaves the stage in a torchlight procession. When we hear Agamemnon speak of the yoke of slavery that Cassandra will have to endure, we think back to the yoke of necessity to which Agamemnon submitted when he sacrificed Iphigeneia, and of the bridle-bolt (a related image) that the Greek army imposed on Troy. Night, through Agamemnon, cast a net on the towers of Troy, and Cassandra is "netted in the toils of destiny", but the net will become the robe in which Agamemnon himself is entangled in his bath as Clytemnestra murders him. In the second play we shall see that metaphorical net when Orestes has it displayed before our eyes. There are recurring images also of wind and storm, of sickness and healing, and of perverted sacrifice. The technique serves at each stage to link the various episodes, and to suggest the causal connection between them.

As for the staging of the play, I single out three of the most striking theatrical moments: (1) Agamemnon, having returned home and made his rather pompous speech to the Chorus, is about to step out of his chariot, with a view to walking up the steps into his palace. At that very moment the great door of the palace opens. As early as the prologue the Watchman had hinted at the dark secrets which lurk behind that door. It has been said that the palace, the building at the back of the stage, is itself almost an actor in this play. So far, only Clytemnestra has used the door. She is the mistress of the house, and no one is allowed to enter it except on her terms. So there she now stands, blocking Agamemnon's entrance to the palace over which he intends to resume the mastery.

(2)   At the end of the same episode we learn what the terms are which will enable him to pass through the door.   Clytemnestra orders her servants to lay out a stream of crimson fabrics or tapestries, all the way from the door to the chariot, and invites her husband to walk over it into the palace. This is often described as the "carpet scene", but that label is misleading.

Carpets are meant to be walked on, and it is abundantly clear, even to Agamemnon himself, that this is not the case now. Quite apart from the waste of very expensive red-dyed fabrics, to trample on such things is not for mortals but for gods. This, presumably, is why Clytemnestra wants him to do it, so that he will incur the resentment of the gods. Agamemnon senses the danger, but in a rapid argument with his wife, allows himself to be persuaded, and the last we see of him is as he walks over the fabrics into the palace, a doomed man. Commentators have been unduly concerned with attempting to explain in psychological terms *why* Agamemnon gives in to Clytemnestra against his better judgement. Some have thought that in his excessive pride he really wants to trample on the fabrics, others that he is a good husband who wants to give his wife what she desires, others again that he is simply the victim of the family-curse. Aeschylus himself, however, does not tell us why he submits, and it is more helpful to concentrate on the complex symbolism which underlies the episode. Firstly, the fabrics, red with the colour of dried blood, clearly symbolise the imminent murder. Out of the palace-door flows a stream of red, physically linking Agamemnon, in his victor's chariot, with the palace in which his blood is about to flow. When Clytemnestra says, "Now, let a path appear, a blood-red river, a triumphal way, and Justice lead him to a home he had not hoped to see", the home which she has in mind is the house of Hades. Secondly, while no one would suppose that he dies *because* he walks on the fabrics, his action does symbolise all his earlier crimes. So far we have *heard* about the sacrifice of Iphigeneia, we have *heard* about the deaths of too many men at Troy and about the sacrilege committed there, but now for the first time we *see* him with our own eyes committing a crime which confirms our feeling that he is about to die and that he deserves to die. Thirdly, Agamemnon's submission to Clytemnestra on this occasion makes visually clear to us his total inferiority to his wife. Clytemnestra, with little difficulty, defeats all of Agamemnon's arguments against walking on the fabrics. "Give in", she says. "If it's by *your* will that you submit, yours is the victory truly". Agamemnon believes her, and departs defeated by the woman. The same door will figure prominently in the second play, in which we shall see Orestes gaining entrance to the palace, and later supplanting his mother as the master of the door. And there too we shall find an argument between a man and a woman, between Orestes and Clytemnestra. But there the situation will be reversed. The man wins the argument, and Orestes leads his mother into the same palace to her death. In all these ways, then, the staging serves to deepen our understanding of Agamemnon's tragedy.

(3)   Clytemnestra, having escorted her husband into the palace, after a worried song from the Chorus comes out again to invite Cassandra to pass through the door. Remember that Cassandra was drawn briefly to our attention immediately before Agamemnon began to walk

over the fabrics, but Aeschylus has kept us waiting to see what her role is to be. Clearly, she can hardly sit there silently in the chariot until the end of the play. Clytemnestra at first tries polite persuasion. She invites Cassandra to come into the palace so that she can share in the celebratory sacrifices for Agamemnon's safe return. She does not explain that Cassandra is to be one of the victims in the sacrifice. Cassandra remains motionless and makes no reply. With splendid illogicality Clytemnestra urges Cassandra, if she cannot understand what she is saying, to use her hands, "communicate in signs". The Chorus add their attempt at persuasion: if Cassandra does not speak Greek, they suggest prosaically, perhaps an interpreter might help. We almost laugh at the contrast between Cassandra's total lack of response and the banality of the Chorus's fussing. But this is not comedy, and the laughter would be nervous laughter. We know that somehow the impasse must be resolved eventually. Cassandra will have to go into the palace to her death. But for the moment Clytemnestra admits defeat and goes back through the great door alone. It is the first, and only, defeat that she suffers in the play, and we may note that it is at the hands of another woman. Left alone with the Chorus Cassandra at last opens her mouth to let out a blood-curdling scream. *Otototoi popoi da*, she cries, words which have resisted the power of translators to render into English. The reason is that they are not really words at all. Rather we should think in terms of a stage-direction: "Cassandra screams loudly and inarticulately". It is a scream which instantly shatters the banality of the Chorus's fussing about the language problem and the need for an interpreter. And it marks the beginning of a remarkable, and highly emotional, scene in which Cassandra will reveal that she requires no such interpreter, as she herself goes on to predict Agamemnon's death and her own, and to interpret herself the present and the future in terms of the past. It is the Chorus which does not understand. When Cassandra at the beginning calls on Apollo, "What have you brought me to? What is this house?", she means, of course, "To what kind of house?", but the Chorus, prosaic as ever, replies by giving the address, "It is the house of the Atreidai, Agamemnon and King Menelaus". Much later in the scene, when the Chorus has a glimmer of understanding that Agamemnon's death is imminent, it asks, "What man is scheming so much suffering?" and Cassandra replies, "So, you've not understood my prophecies". That scream, with its sudden change of mood, is one of the greatest screams in the history of the theatre.

Finally, I turn to the characterisation of Clytemnestra. Aristotle in his *Poetics* rightly tells us that in Greek tragedy characterisation is always subordinate to plot. In other words the plot is not created as a vehicle for preconceived characters. Rather, the characterisation serves to explain why the characters act and react in the way that they do. Some plots will require more fully developed characterisation than others. So, in *Agamemnon* we need to know what it is that makes Agamemnon give in to his wife, and what it is that makes her the powerful figure that she is. The result is that in Clytemnestra we have one of the most towering figures in all Greek tragedy. She is introduced to us first, as we saw, by the Watchman in the prologue, with his description of her as "the one who has a man's brain in a woman's body", and, when she comes forward at the end of the Chorus's entrance-song, it is in terms of her power that the Chorus address her. Throughout the play she demonstrates her power over, and her ability to manipulate, one character after another. Only in Cassandra does she meet her match, but Cassandra is another woman, and her victory over Clytemnestra is only temporary. All the other characters are men. The characterisation of the tragic chorus is often comparatively unimportant, but in this play the consistent weakness of the Chorus is vital, not for its own sake, but for what it tells us about the strength of Clytemnestra. When, at the end of the song that started off as a song of victory and thanksgiving, the Chorus turn to wishful thinking, hoping that the war is not over after all, they comfort themselves with the thought that it was only a woman who gave them the news, and, as everyone knows, one cannot trust what a woman tells one. Without realising it, it is the Chorus of men, who, by indulging in irrational wishful-thinking, are behaving in the way that a male Greek audience would no doubt expect women to behave. In the Cassandra scene it is the woman who understands, while the Chorus again are unable to grasp her meaning, or rather they do not want to grasp it because they find it too horrific to contemplate. Then, when they hear Agamemnon's offstage death-cries, the Chorus wonder whether to intervene, but we are not surprised that they decide to do nothing. They are too weak even to go through the palace-door, which, as we remember, is controlled by Clytemnestra. In their entrance song the Chorus introduced themselves as old men, physically weak, past the age of military service. But is has become clear that they are also morally and intellectually weak. Only at the very end of the play do the Chorus surprise us by being prepared to take on Aegisthus and his bodyguard in a fight. But Aegisthus is another *man*, and the Chorus's readiness to fight him is an indication of *his* weakness, as is the fact that he needs a bodyguard in the first place. Clytemnestra required no such bodyguard. She has dominated through the sheer power of her personality. In the final lines of the play, when Clytemnestra invites her lover to join her in wielding power within the palace, we can be in little doubt as to who will be the dominant partner in the relationship. In this play, then, all the men behave like the Greeks' traditional idea of women, while the two women, but particularly Clytemnestra, are strong like traditional men. It would be tempting to see it as some kind of early feminist tract. But the temptation should probably be resisted. Aeschylus, in his male-dominated society, certainly intends us to understand the reversal of gender roles as a sign of a perversion in Argive society. In *Eumenides*, the third part of the trilogy, normal order will be restored when, at the trial of Orestes before the court of the Areopagus in Athens, Apollo argues that the killing of one's husband is a worse crime than the murder of one's mother. Orestes will be acquitted, and he will depart for Argos to take up the kingship and to exercise his male power. Yet, doubts remain even at the end. Apollo is not a particularly convincing character in that play, and Orestes is acquitted only because the votes of the jurors are equal. Clytemnestra's brief appearance at the beginning of the play as a ghost will remind us of the powerful woman whom we have seen in the first two plays. It is hard to find anything to admire in Agamemnon, but, despite the enormity of her crime, there are many who will continue to admire Clytemnestra.

Heroic Agamemnon

Carmel McCallum-Barry

> ...villains by necessity; fools by
> heavenly compulsion
> Shakespeare, *King Lear* I.2,132

Over the last one hundred and fifty years
Aeschylus' *Agamemnon* has been the subject of
a vast amount of scholarly discussion, much of
which focuses on determining the nature and
extent of his guilt. For what reasons does he
deserve to be killed by his wife when he returns
as a victorious general? Perhaps everything
possible has already been said on this point, but
the fact that new translations and stagings
continue to be produced demonstrates that re-
examination of Agamemnon's character and
situation offers a valid way of looking at some
problems of decision making and conduct that is
still of interest. The *Millennium Project* currently
under way in the United States lists almost 50
commercial productions or adaptations of
Agamemnon or of the *Oresteia* trilogy between
1966 and 2001. This period starts in a time of
intense debate over the war in Vietnam and
covers American military involvement in several
other arenas such as the Persian Gulf and the
Balkans; clearly *Agamemnon* can be seen as a
way of addressing issues concerning war and
personal responsibility, as well as gender issues.
So it is worth trying to establish what aspects of
the play have contributed to the relevance of the

play for translators, directors and audiences, and I concentrate here on the portrayal of the king who gives his name to the play.

Modern perceptions of the character of Agamemnon are not on the whole favourable, a man who sacrifices his daughter in order to embark on a war does not find a sympathetic audience today and his standing as a tragic hero is not high. Can we even call him a hero in the play called for him? The acting role is really a minor one, as he is on scene for just under one tenth of the drama. He does not appear in person until halfway through the play (810); very soon he enters the palace to be murdered by his wife (957). Although we are given a vivid picture of him by the chorus well before his appearance neither this nor his brief scene with Clytemnestra manages to engage our sympathies; he appears as a brutal warlord, relishing the destruction he has brought about in Troy, crassly blind to warnings from the chorus, arrogant, rude and disparaging to his wife. Indeed it is she, Clytemnestra, who truly dominates both the action and the actors in this play.

In general our culture disposes us to value individual family needs over the demands of the state so we are ready to recognise the rights and feelings of a wife and mother in Clytemnestra's situation and even to consider her revenge justified. It is not therefore surprising that many recent interpretations see her as the hero of the play and condemn Agamemnon as a man who

44

could bring himself to kill his own daughter. However, we stand at great distance from the Athenians who first saw *Agamemnon*, not just in time, but in cultural and ethical expectations, and should not forget that in the last play of the *Oresteia* it is made clear by Apollo, representing Zeus and the established order, that the killing of Agamemnon by his wife, not his sacrifice of their daughter, is the most serious of the three intrafamilial killings that the trilogy explores. In making judgements about Agamemnon we make them from a modern viewpoint which tends to see the sacrifice of an innocent child by her father in order to start a war as a greater crime than the murder of a husband by his wife.

However it is clear that even early in the modern period the presentation of a king sacrificing his daughter did not have the same emotional impact that it has for us today. In 1553 Lady Lumley made an English translation of *Iphigeneia at Aulis* (Euripides' version of the sacrifice), which, amazingly, she dedicated to her father, an important and extremely adroit political player in the state councils of Edward VI, Mary and Elizabeth. If we accept that the notion of self-sacrifice in state service was not inimical to the thinking of these great dynastic families, it may help us realise that some accommodation is necessary between ancient and modern views of Agamemnon's character and function in the trilogy.

In fact it is in relation to his dilemma over the

sacrifice of Iphigeneia that he can be called a tragic hero; his situation is typical of what has been called "the highest type of tragedy", concerned with problems that are insoluble and where the character is entangled in toils from which there is no escape. Necessity compels Agamemnon to make a choice which is no choice, he asks himself, "how can I desert the ships, the alliance?", but there is no real possibility of doing this.

However there are other aspects of the characterisation of Agamemnon in the play which show him in an unfavourable light, aspects which are clearly signalled by the text and so can be assumed to have resonance for Aeschylus' primary audience as well as subsequent ones. I mean here his harsh brutality when describing the destruction of Troy, his failure to understand the warnings of the chorus even though he insists that he does, and of course his behaviour towards his wife. These aspects taken together work to undermine his standing as a hero in a way that his sacrifice of Iphigeneia does not. His blindness to the chorus's warnings and his defeat in debate by the woman he disparages show him not only as weak willed but even stupid. His heroic persona as king and warrior is at odds with his changeable, often disastrously inconsistent, behaviour towards others.

I want to suggest that this ambiguous characterisation of Agamemnon as a man who somehow misses 'great hero' status despite his position as the lord of Mycenae and supreme army commander is what makes him, as Vernant says, 'good to think with'. And his suitability for exploring the issues that such a character raises is not confined to modern interpreters; the characterisation of Agamemnon in this play agrees with the view we get of him in the mythical tradition and other literature. The issues in question are familiar, and recur frequently in Greek literature until the end of the classical period. They concern conflicts in relationships within the household (*oikos*) and on a larger scale between the claims of individual households and those of the state. Such tensions are commonly enacted through examination of the role of women in the household and their contribution to the well-being or dissolution of their *oikos*. As a man who has on the one hand responsibilities of state, a war to wage and an army to co-ordinate, and on the other a transgressive sister in law (Helen), children and a wife who feels he has insulted her as both wife and mother, Agamemnon can provide a variety of problematical situations to think about.

Besides looking at the presentation of Agamemnon in Aeschylus, I also want to glance briefly at some of his other appearances in Greek literature (Homer and Euripides) which should make clear that his failings as we see them in Aeschylus are part of a consistent character portrayal.

In this play we first hear of Agamemnon from the chorus of older men left behind when the army sailed for Troy to avenge the abduction of Helen. They think back to the time ten years earlier as the expedition was setting out. Their version of what happened is told vividly, but allusively; causes of events and actions are not always clear, nor are the chorus's views of those actions. However we are expressly told that Zeus, king of the gods, sends the brothers against Troy and gives them a favourable omen to show approval; as the troops assemble two eagles are seen to kill and devour a pregnant hare and her young. The prophet Calchas recognises that the two eagles represent the two brother kings who in time will devour the city of Troy. But the goddess of wild nature, Artemis, 'hates the eagles' feast' (137) and Calchas fears she may strike at the army to stop it sailing and demand another killing to cause strife within the house. The chorus thus anticipates the action of the play and sees that the sacrifice demanded (Iphigeneia) means that Clytemnestra will be waiting for her revenge. At this point they break off their disturbing recollections and address Zeus directly, which reminds us how closely the god is involved; he has sent the brothers after their revenge, the expedition is his will. This point made, the old men return to the scene at Aulis where the Greek fleet is unable to sail because of adverse winds. The prophet, blaming Artemis, announces a 'cure'; Agamemnon must sacrifice his daughter Iphigeneia. The king realises the horror of his position; heavy his fate if he disobeys but heavy also if he slaughters his child. Aeschylus makes him expand on the horror, in language which is harsh and emotive. Iphigeneia is 'the glory of our house'; he will be 'defiling a father's hands with streams of virgin's blood'. He does not spare himself or the audience: 'which of these actions is without evils?'(206-217). The second course of action, to desert the ships and allies, he mentions only to conclude that the angry goddess's demand for blood in return for the sailing of the ships is right (*themis*). At this point the chorus move from the imaginative recreation of the scene at Aulis to a narrative of what happened next (from vivid present to past tenses, 217-227). Agamemnon 'put on the yokestrap of necessity', that is, he bowed to an unavoidable compulsion. Once he did this, 'he changed his thinking' and cruelly and shamefully sacrificed his daughter as a preliminary rite for the expedition. This is usually understood to mean that he acted abnormally, that insanity (*parakopa*) took over. The account of the sacrifice is vivid and terrifying, easily arousing pity for the helpless Iphigeneia, but it worked, the 'cure' was effective and the Greeks were able to sail for Troy. Aeschylus makes very clear the brutal nastiness of the sacrifice, but nevertheless we are told that the demand for it was considered justified and that all the leaders agreed. Agamemnon had to do it and after he gave in to necessity he was out of his mind in the doing of the deed.

Most modern scholars agree on these points - that Zeus sends Agamemnon against Troy and that the expedition and demand for sacrifice (not the sacrifice itself) are considered 'right'. Later in the play Cassandra, in her prophetic vision of Agamemnon's murder sees as the reasons for his death both the crimes of his ancestors and Clytemnestra's anger because Agamemnon has brought home a mistress. She says nothing of the death of Iphigeneia; Apollo, who inspires her, apparently does not consider it a factor leading to Agamemnon's punishment. Only Clytemnestra identifies his sacrifice of their daughter as one of the reasons why he deserves to be killed. As in the trilogy as a whole the male gods give approval to the actions of male characters; Clytemnestra's female viewpoint is not relevant for decisions of state importance.

At no point in the play is it suggested that he can send away the army; other Greek dramatists take a similar view. In Sophocles' *Electra* it is implied that the army would refuse to obey such a command; in *Iphigeneia at Aulis* the army is prepared to attack anyone who would put off the sacrifice. We can therefore disregard the sacrifice as a factor working to diminish or lower his character, it involves a tragic choice such as many heroes have to make and Agamemnon is involved against his will, forced by necessity, as both ancients and moderns agree.

With reference to the chorus's account of the sacrifice of his daughter he is a tragic hero, involved against his will through no fault of his own (like Oedipus). It is in his personal appearance on scene that Agamemnon loses credibility. The chorus salute him as conqueror of

Troy but warn him not to be deceived by others (i.e. Clytemnestra) who may greet him joyously but in reality are his enemies. His answer seems to ignore what has just been said (810-854). First he gives thanks to the gods for his victory, the gods who, he says, are jointly responsible (*metaitioi*) with him for the destruction of Troy. His account of that destruction makes us recoil; like his words at the sacrifice quoted by the chorus earlier, it is brutal and insensitive. The gods voted to destroy the city by casting their votes in 'a bloodstained urn'; 'the beast of Argos ground the city into dust....for the sake of a woman'. He says too that he knows how to distinguish between true and false friends and will take counsel to settle the troubles in the city, but no thought of trouble in his own house seems to have crossed his mind. This impression of the warleader as both brutal and crass is reinforced in the central scene with Clytemnestra. Her speech to greet him, a wonderful piece of publicity for herself as a faithful wife, mainly addresses the chorus who know very well that she has taken Aegisthus as her lover and minder. Only at the end does she turn to her husband insisting that the conqueror of Troy should not walk on the ground, but on the red dyed cloths that her women spread for him. He replies abruptly, even rudely. Her speech is like his absence, "stretched out too long"; her praises are excessive; he refuses her offer of precious cloths to walk on, as if he were a decadent barbarian and asks only for the reverence suited to a man, not a god. Agamemnon's initial response to the idea of treading on the cloths is a very proper one, rejecting the temptation to arrogance and pride, but of course as the scene develops he changes his mind, outmanoeuvred by Clytemnestra's arguments. He takes off his shoes to walk upon the cloths hoping to minimise an action he still feels to be wrong, ashamed "to ruin the house under my feet, destroying its wealth" (948,9). There is a clear parallel here with the sacrifice of Iphigeneia, where he has to destroy the child he calls "the glory of our house". On both occasions he is compelled by outside forces to do something he feels is wrong.

One cannot deny that Agamemnon's shortcomings are clearly flagged in the play, but he is no more guilty of crime than Clytemnestra or their son Orestes, who with a similar tragic choice to make, returns in the next play of the trilogy to kill his mother. Orestes is forgiven his murder and allowed to return to normal society mainly because he has avenged his father, a ruling male who was shamefully killed by a woman. Agamemnon is no more arrogant and peremptory towards Clytemnestra than Sophocles' Ajax is towards his wife. The point is that other personages of Greek myth and poetry act in similar ways to Agamemnon without detracting from their heroic status, but he is repeatedly presented as less than heroic. His personality problem is not a creation of Aeschylus, but is consistent with his appearances in Homer and the other dramatists.

In the *Iliad* where the famous heroes are defined,

we already can recognise his ambivalent qualities. He is of course leader of the army who "rules over more men"; he is also given his place in the limelight as a warrior in Book 11, where his heroic exploits on the battlefield form the main subject matter. But at the same time his inadequacies as a commander show up in his disastrous handling of personalities who have their own claims to honour. The cause of the action of the *Iliad* is the quarrel between Agamemnon and Achilles, the greatest Greek warrior. At the command of Apollo and in order to save the Greek army from plague, Agamemnon hands back to her father the woman Chryseis, part of his war booty, (even though he says he rates her before his wife Clytemnestra, I.113). However he feels that his status as leader has been diminished and demands another woman in compensation. Achilles objects to Agamemnon's selfish greed and the two men explode in angry exchange. The result is that Agamemnon takes for himself Achilles' prize, the woman Briseis and Achilles withdraws from the fighting, threatening to return home. His withdrawal is the beginning of disaster for the Greeks and Agamemnon soon regrets his actions and is ready to conciliate Achilles for the good of the army as a whole. It is significant that, when Achilles eventually accepts his apology and agrees to fight again, both he and the rest of the Greeks accept that Agamemnon was 'not himself' when he quarrelled with Achilles, but acted under the influence of *Ate*, blind folly sent by the gods. It is interesting to see this explanation in parallel with

53

his change of mind and personality when he comes to sacrifice Iphigeneia. In his dealings with other heroes (e.g. his words to Odysseus and Diomedes in *Iliad* 4. 349-400) we see a familiar pattern of behaviour. In the heat of the moment he speaks insulting words which he quickly regrets and soon has to apologise for hasty judgements; again we see traces of the Aeschlyean Agamemnon who fails to think carefully before he speaks to the chorus and to his wife.

Our view of Agamemnon so far is of a rather insecure army commander, who sets aside family concerns for the greater good of his army and his own career ambitions. He is not good at personal relations at work or at home and often has to change his mind. He takes a mistress (twice) and is foolishly disparaging of his wife, but in the battle on this front his wife gets the better of him and compels him to act in ways that she has determined.

There is no mention of a young girl's sacrifice in Homer, but it and the other ingredients just mentioned recur in the characterisation of Agamemnon in Euripides' *Hecuba* (before 423 BC). It is set in the Greek camp after the fall of Troy, and Polyxena, daughter of Hecuba, once queen of Troy, is sacrificed to honour the spirit of the dead Achilles. In this play Agamemnon is not associated with the sacrifice of the innocent girl and in fact expresses his pity for Hecuba, allowing her to take charge of the burial although she is now a slave with no rights; Euripides allows him to redeem himself in retrospect. But Hecuba also wants to avenge her son, killed by one of the Greek allies, and goes to work upon Agamemnon who is clearly not able to stand up to her arguments. Although he refuses to exact punishment himself as he fears the Greek army would disapprove, he allows Hecuba to take her own vengeance. Here we have a rewriting of Agamemnon's guilt over virgin sacrifices, which absolves him of blame in the case of Polyxena, while his other character traits remain the same. As in Aeschylus he is concerned for the opinions of the army and cannot withstand a forceful matriarch; when it comes to debate he is no match for such women.

Euripides returns to Agamemnon and his family in *Iphigeneia at Aulis*, (produced after 406 BC). This is a much more comprehensive view of the motivation and responsibility not just of Agamemnon but of everyone with an interest in the sacrifice - other members of the family and the army that is waiting to sail. The play begins with Agamemnon changing his mind, a telling comment. He had at first agreed to sacrifice his daughter and summoned her on the pretext that she was to be married to Achilles, but he now sends a second message telling Clytemnestra not to bring their daughter to Aulis after all. The letter is intercepted by Menelaus who harshly criticises his brother's desertion of the Greek cause in favour of his family; the argument between the brothers evaluates the kind of leader that Agamemnon has been (fickle and changeable), and the very personal family grievances that caused and are caused by the war (Helen going off to Troy with Paris, need for Iphigeneia's sacrifice). Agamemnon's anguish at the thought of killing his child leads Menelaus to change his mind also - he can get another wife. But it is too late as his wife and daughter have already arrived. The meeting of Agamemnon and Iphigeneia displays a loving father-daughter relationship, its sentimentality ironically subverted by the fact that the language, which for Iphigeneia refers to marriage, is for Agamemnon the language of sacrificial death. When she discovers the truth she at first pleads for her life, but strangely changes her mind, deciding to die voluntarily for the success of the expedition, which she equates with the salvation of Greece from barbarians. Clytemnestra is also sympathetically portrayed in this play as a doting mother who has also been a model wife. She wins sympathy and establishes a righteous motive for the murder of her husband. If he sacrifices their daughter to go to war, how will she feel sitting at home looking at the child's empty chair? Why not take Helen's daughter instead of his loyal wife's?

Euripides makes no judgement on any one person in this play, all must take some share of blame, including the people as a whole, that is, the army. The mob is eager for war at any cost, a war to get back an unfaithful wife and we are left to think carefully about the morality of such a situation.

In Homer and in the drama of the fifth century we find an Agamemnon we should feel sorry for. He is conscientious although often ineffective in his capacity as leader of the people, and fails conspicuously to deal with individuals and their needs. It is noticeable that he is constantly perceived or defined in relation to females, especially in contexts where women's prerogatives and conduct within the family are in question. It is obvious that he cannot deal properly with his own *oikos* and the women responsible for its continuance. Helen dishonoured the *oikos* of his brother Menelaus; to rectify this Agamemnon went to war, sacrificing his own daughter. On his return he insulted his wife by bringing home a mistress and telling Clytemnestra to treat her well. Cassandra herself sees the connections quite clearly. As she goes in to her death she asks to be remembered by the chorus "when a woman (Clytemnestra) dies in return for a women (Cassandra) and another man (Aegisthus) falls in return for the man so badly married" (Agamemnon). If he cannot manage his own house well it is no surprise that Agamemnon's handling of the larger society of his fellow chieftains is equally disastrous, and this is why the play can speak so often to different audiences. Agamemnon's exercise of power is seriously flawed on the domestic, military and diplomatic fronts, and we always need ways to question the workings of authority.

Agamemnon

Jasper Griffin

In Athens everything was competitive; anthropologists call it an agonistic culture. When the Athenians put on plays, it seemed natural that the event should take the form of a competition, with prizes for playwrights and also for performers. As it was also a religious occasion, part of the festival in honour of the god Dionysus, it seems to have been felt that nobody should be judged to have simply lost; so the three playwrights received first, second and third prize. Each poet entered three tragic plays and, at the end, a more rumbustious performance called a satyr play, in which the chorus consisted of a group of those lewd, inquisitive, and frivolous beings, the half human satyrs.

The three tragedies are called a trilogy. In the first half of the fifth century trilogies often possessed a unity: the plays dealt with successive points in a single story, or in the history of a single family. Later on the fashion changed, and both Sophocles and Euripides regularly entered sets of three essentially unrelated plays, with no continuity of story or characters. Only one trilogy has come down to us complete, the Orestes trilogy (*Oresteia*) of Aeschylus, of which *Agamemnon* is the first play. In addition to its own merits - Swinburne called it "the greatest creation of the human mind" - the *Oresteia* has the extra interest of being our chief source for understanding the early history of tragedy itself.

Many hundreds of plays were staged in Athens in the fifth century. We have only a few of them. With one exception, all those we have dramatise a story from the myths. That was evidently not a rule, (Aeschylus' *Persians* deals with the very recent invasion of Greece by the Persian King Xerxes and its defeat), but it was felt to be appropriate. The reason seems to have been that in the myths, and above all the myths as they are treated in the great epics of Homer, events are presented not simply as "something that happened", but as an intelligible picture of the interplay of human and divine action and causation. In the *Iliad* and *Odyssey* the world is transparent, allowing us to see the activity of the gods, as they intervene in the lives and achievements of men and women. The human actors are themselves closer to the gods than later people felt themselves to be, and in many cases they are the off-spring of a god or (more rarely) a goddess.

The Trojan War involved the gods very directly. Gods schemed and even fought on both sides. Since the sin of Paris had started the whole story, the eventual fall of Troy exemplified the progress and punishment of human presumption and folly. It also shows us what it is to be human. In the *Iliad* we meet and sympathise with the wives and children of the Trojans, especially Hector's wife Andromache and their baby son Astyanax: the child will be killed, and his mother enslaved, when the city falls. The innocent must suffer, and the agents of justice must do fearful things. At the end of the poem Achilles, the greatest Greek hero, and old Priam, king of Troy, come together, over the body of Priam's son Hector, slain by Achilles, and in the shadow of Achilles' own foreknown death. They share a moment of tragic insight and tragic intensity, as together they contemplate the hard doom of human kind.

When the Trojan prince Paris carried off the wife of his Greek host, King Menelaus, he offended against a cardinal rule of Greek ethics. Agamemnon, Menelaus' brother, was the most powerful king in Greece, in some sense the superior of the other chieftains, and he summoned all Greece to punish Troy and bring back the abducted Queen Helen. At the opening of the play it is ten years since the great armada sailed away from Greece. We are in Argos, King Agamemnon's capital, outside his palace, awaiting news. It is very early in the morning, a time at which many Greek tragedies are set - the spectators arrived early and watched the plays out of doors, in the great theatre hewn out of the rock of the Acropolis, below where the Parthenon (not yet built) now stands.

A watchman sets the scene. Posted by the Queen, Clytemnestra, a woman of whom he says that she has "a man's will in a woman's body", he is filled with gloom and apprehension. He longs for his King's return, but something is wrong; he dares not say more.   Suddenly he sees the distant beacon: Troy has fallen! He cries out in joy; but, as so often in the play, joy turns at once to apprehension. "This house, this building, if it could but speak..." It is the cue for the entry of the chorus, a regular feature of Greek tragedy, a collective group who accompany and interpret the action by their songs and their dancing. In this play they are old gentlemen, too old already ten years ago to go to Troy, and their dancing will not be lively; they support themselves on sticks, and they call themselves "a mirage shimmering in the light of day". They enter marching, their thoughts fixed on the outbreak of the war, "Ten years ago..." They review the King's departure and the role of Zeus, supreme god, in ordering it.

Their thoughts become darker.   Before Agamemnon and the fleet could sail for Troy, a dreadful thing happened. Becalmed, windless, the army saw a repulsive sight: two eagles tore a pregnant hare to pieces.   Calchas the priest interpreted the sinister omen: the eagles stand for the two brother kings, and their act is the act of Agamemnon: he will kill the innocent children of Troy - and there is something in heaven which will make him pay. The price is the sacrifice of his own child, the young princess Iphigeneia.

The King wriggled: "if I pollute these hands, her father's hands..." But in the end he submits, feebly hoping that it may be for the best. They cut her throat as if she were a sheep, an ordinary sacrificial victim. The tableau of the helpless girl, gagged and unable to speak, appealing with her eyes to the assembled kings, who knew her and had listened to her singing in her father's house, is meant to be one of ultimate horror. Then, after a pitiless build-up which leaves nothing to our imagination, the chorus say grimly, "What happened next I cannot say - I did not see it. But Calchas' visions come to pass."

The choral song is very long and very powerful. It presents the act of Agamemnon, and the sack of Troy, as both the justified punishment of sin, demanded by Heaven, and simultaneously an act of appalling horror. Human sacrifice, though it occurs in the myths, was profoundly alien to the practice of the Greeks of the classical period.

The song also contains dark warnings, couched in oracular language, that there may be waiting at home a "governess that guards the house, the child-avenging Fury which will not forget." The language is deliberately ambiguous, in the manner of oracles, between a supernatural agent of vengeance and the resentful bereaved wife, who will avenge the death of her child. It means both; and the guilty wife will tell the accusing chorus, before the end of the play: "Are you so sure I was his wife? Are you so sure I did it? No. The atavistic demon of revenge, the wraith, has become flesh..."

The Queen, so long invisible and unresponsive behind the palace door, now enters. She informs the expectant chorus of the fall of Troy. It seems that she alone knows of the chain of beacons which have passed on the news in blazing triumph, leaping from crag to crag: and she can describe, as if by second sight, the scenes of slaughter in the fallen city. "And if", she says insincerely, "they reverence the gods of Troy, the sanctuaries still sacred to the gods though Troy is taken, the victors may yet stop the cycle and escape defeat." Her command of the situation is sinister and compelling.

The chorus sing a song of meditation. What has befallen Troy is a blow from Zeus; that at least one can make out. The gods really do punish the guilty! They go on to consider the guilt of Troy, the abduction of Helen. Divine temptation, which looks so attractive, lures men on to their destruction. So it was when Helen passed so lightly through the gates of Troy, the city which she would ruin, amid prophecies of disaster. Ares, god of war, is a money-changer of bodies; in exchange for the man you knew, what you get back is an urn containing his ashes. The casualty lists are building up resentment at home in Greece, and a ruler who is hated must pay a price; better to avoid dangerous prominence. "A lack of envy - that (for me) is wealth. *I* have no wish to sack a city."

A sailor enters, with news. Troy has fallen indeed, and the King is close at hand; but it soon emerges - again that change from apparent joy to gloom - that at the sack of Troy the shrines of the gods have, as Clytemnestra hoped, been profaned and ruined. And the fleet has suffered on the way home from a storm, the Aegean Sea is "blossoming with corpses", and Menelaus is lost, none knows where. That inauspicious ending leads into the third choral song. The name Helen: Hell for men - it must have been Hades ("someone whom we could not see", an etymology of his name) who named her so appropriately. Her charm has ruined Troy. Even so might a man rear a lion cub, charming and appealing in its infancy, but a bringer of death by and by.

When Helen went to Troy, the Trojans felt a mood of voluptuous enjoyment, she was so beautiful; but she made them change their soft music to funeral dirges, and brides wept for the death of their men.

> An old saying:
> > *Great wealth grown fat does not die childless,*
> > *no, good fortune breeds destruction, all insatiate.*
> I don't agree.
> *I* think that crime breeds crime in its own image, multiplied.

> But Justice can blaze bright in smoky cottages,
> radiant for those whose lives are pure.
> She turns her face from glittering prizes,
> superficial,
> golden-plated, groped by dirty hands, and
> goes.
> Modesty attracts her, never wealth,
> so counterfeit, so fraudulent, so flattering.
> So, Justice steers all things to their conclusion.

Agamemnon! King!

We have seen those dirty hands before: King Agamemnon spoke so of his own hands, when he assented to his daughter's death. It is in that sinister light that the King and Conqueror appears and is greeted by his loyal subjects. He is drawn in a chariot, in which another figure is standing, as far as possible concealed from the gaze of the audience.

He greets his house and his gods, says that he has heard disquieting rumours, and declares that "Where there's need for remedy, for cure, then we shall try to stop the cancer spreading - with the surgeon's knife or cauterising fire". But he will not be quick enough. He makes to enter the house; but the door opens, and Clytemnestra, who has been invisible during his speech, appears in the door and blocks his way. She has a speech to make, and a long one; "matching my absence: both too long", Agamemnon will say. It is addressed, not to him, but to the people of Argos. She has heard so many messages of bad news from the army at Troy! She so often attempted suicide! As for infidelity, she knows no more of that than of the art of dipping metal. "And if my husband had sustained as many wounds as their reports came home to me, I swear he'd have more gashes in him than a hunting net. And if he'd died as many deaths as men reported, he would be another, a second Trinity, so often resurrected, slain..." We are to remember those phrases, when she appears exultant after his murder, having thrown a net over him and dipped her sword thoroughly, stabbing him thrice. She announces her deadly purpose, barely veiled, confident that she can get away with it.

She concludes with a flurry of Oriental fulsomeness, culminating in the order that the foot of the man who took Troy should not touch the earth but step on the rich tapestries which she now lays down for him to walk over; and as he advances she gets down on her knees in the oriental gesture of grovelling which the Greeks hated. It is done to make him look bad; look like an Asiatic despot, who has forgotten his human limitations. Agamemnon is uneasy; the atmosphere is not to his liking; he tries to evade performing an action which by its wanton abuse of precious things is calculated to attract the indignation of heaven; but she beats him, and off the stage he goes, removing his shoes and feebly hoping that no divine eye is watching. The episode serves several purposes. It presents in transposed form the struggle of husband and wife; it shows her as the stronger, so that her victory represents his killing; and it shows him again in the situation of agonised choice, forced to perform an action which he knows will be distasteful to heaven, unable to escape it, and feebly hoping for the best.

The Queen watches him go, walking up a stream of rich crimson stuff, the colour of blood, as if the guilt of the house were leaking out visibly before our eyes. "Zeus, Zeus, you who bring all things to fulflment", she prays, "now fulfil my prayers". And she follows him in. We expect, after this build-up, that the next thing will be the King's death. The chorus sing a song of foreboding. "Why is this horror with me always, roosting, glowering grim, and beating its black wings against my heart to lash my prophecies? Once a man's black blood, man's dying blood, has fallen on the earth, what cures are there, what chants can call it back again?" But we get a surprise. Clytemnestra comes out of the house again, to summon in the second figure in the chariot, from whom until now Aeschylus has been careful to divert our attention. It is a woman: the Trojan princess Cassandra, brought home as Agamemnon's prize and concubine.

The Queen invites her in; she does not respond. The Queen gives up and leaves. Now Cassandra begins to utter. At first it is in short lyric cries of despair, which the chorus cannot understand. Gradually she settles down to more normal speech, as the chorus, unnerved by her hints, pass into lyric song, so that the scene has a musical shape: she passes from song to speech, they from speech to song. The foreign woman shows her power as a prophetess, given her by Apollo, in return for the promise of sexual favours; but then she broke her word, and in consequence her prophetic utterances are never believed.

First she detects the haunting scent of murder in the atmosphere of the palace: murder, yes, and cannibalism; it is the crime of Agamemnon's father Atreus, who avenged his brother's seduction of his wife by killing his brother's children and serving their flesh to him to eat. The chorus are shocked, oppressed, shaken. Agamemnon the killer of his daughter Iphigenia, we reflect, is the son of a killer of children; and now he has caused the death of the children of Troy. The pattern is complete. At last Cassandra predicts in clear language the murder of the King. "I too shall die. I only pray that when I'm dead you'll be my witness, when she dies for me, a woman dying for a woman's sake, and when a man falls for a man so cruelly wedded." And she goes off, to her death. A slave, a foreign woman, at the bottom of the heap, she succeeds in comprehending her fate and accepting it, where the great King Agamemnon, godsent conqueror, went to his doom in helpless incomprehension. The cutting contrast is meant to be felt.

Her prophecy brings out the parallel, which we had missed, of the killing of Agamemnon and Cassandra with the killing, in requital, of Clytemnestra and her paramour Aegisthus, sole survivor of those murdered children of Atreus' brother. It will be brought out visually: this play ends with the display of the bodies of a man and a woman; the next play, *Choephoroe*, will end with the identical tableau. That is more than an effective piece of spectacle. It also shows that the crime of Clytemnestra and the vengeance of her son Orestes, which was meant to be so different and to put an end to the cycle of killings, have a horrid resemblance. The story cannot, after all, end there.

At last it is almost a relief to hear the scream of Agamemnon as he is killed. The chorus debate what to do, and they do nothing. The house opens, and the Queen appears, standing over the body she has killed. She utters a speech of unmatched brutality and power. "What I have done is done, and I shall not disown it. The all enclosing net, drag-net of destiny - I cast its fabric and its wealth of ruin round him. I strike two blows and with two groans upon this very place he lets his limbs fall limp. And on his fallen body I bestow a third, an offering of thanks long prayed for to Zeus, the Guardian of the Dead, who rules beneath the earth. And so he lies there, ebbing out the vomit of his very life, and gasping forth a frothing arc of blood he spatters me with dark dank droplets of his bloody dew, while I exulted as the growing corn exults, in labour with the bursting seed, when Zeus sends down his rain." The chorus are apparently more shocked by her speech than by her crime: "How can you speak like this, so brazenly? How can you boast that you've killed your own husband?" There follows a scene, in which they accuse her and denounce her act, while she defends herself and attacks the dead man.

Who now will bury him?
Who will lament him?
Will you dare to do it,
    to rasp out a requiem for the husband you
    killed?

"Don't worry," comes the implacable reply, "Iphigeneia will welcome him, a daughter welcoming a father, stretching out her arms, cool, incorporeal, kissing him in lingering embrace." A taunt in answer to a taunt! The chorus are forced to admit that there is some justice on her side; but still, she will pay for her crime. Crime and Punishment: that is the Law.

At last her lover Aegisthus appears. A low and blustering character, where she is daemonic and possessed of a dark grandeur, he threatens the chorus with violence. It looks as if a physical clash is imminent, but the Queen brushes it aside with contempt. There have been enough violent actions, she tells Aegisthus; no need for more. We see clearly how much she is the stronger. On that note of unresolved discord the play ends. It is, we remind ourselves, the first of a set of three. In the second, her son Orestes, ordered by Apollo at his shrine of Delphi, avenges his father by killing his mother. The Furies which such an act evokes drive him in crazed terror over the face of the earth.

In the third play Orestes comes to Athens, where the purification of blood guilt, which mere rituals were powerless to achieve, is brought about by a rational argument and democratic vote. Athens is that new thing, a democracy, and a jury of the citizens judges his case. By the narrowest possible margin, he is acquitted. The Furies, by now hideously visible, threaten Athens with plague and sterility, but in the end they are talked round and accept an honoured place in the community, to which deterrent terror, in its proper place, makes a vital contribution. We see that a minority must accept the results of a vote, however narrow. Equally, when Athena, for all her strength, refuses to use threats, and insists on arguing with the Furies until she persuades them, we see that the majority must respect a minority and not "trample it under the hoofs of its horses", in the image which the Furies use repeatedly.

The trilogy deals with deep problems of guilt and responsibility. Can a sin like that of Troy be punished, without the punisher in his turn committing horrendous crimes? (We might think of the morality of bombing the German cities in the last War.) What are the effects of a bad heredity? It is somehow natural that the son of a child-killer should find himself killing children, including his own. Who is the parent: mother or father? With which should the child side? What should be the relation of the sexes? We see a woman too masculine, while her paramour, who leaves the killing to her and threatens the old men of the chorus afterwards, is insultingly called a woman. Their unnatural ascendancy threatens the community with servitude on the political level, and with barrenness from the side of offended deities. In the third play gods of the upper world (Apollo, Athena) clash with gods of the earth (Furies).

The two prophetic figures, Calchas and Cassandra, one of either sex, bring in a vein of oracular language, with animal imagery. Agamemnon and Menelaus are like two eagles lamenting the loss of their young; the reception of guilty Helen by Troy is like the rearing of a lion cub in one's house; Cassandra sees the killing of Agamemnon by his wife as a bull being gored by the cow; or, again, he is like the noble lion, whose mate has in his absence bedded with the wolf. In the second play the Queen has a dream of the return of her son: she has suckled a serpent at the breast, which bites her and draws blood. And so on.

The animal imagery is not an externally applied poetical decoration. The world of the *Oresteia* is one in which the borders which separate the human from the divine, on the one side, and from the animal, on the other, are permeable. We are permitted to see through them. We share the special vision of Cassandra, who can detect ancient crime and see a pattern in it, or of Calchas, proclaiming that the price of killing the children of Troy is the killing of one's own child. Nightmares, omens, prophecies, and supernatural agents, tempting and punishing and employing terror as their weapon, make up an atmosphere like that of *Macbeth*.

The shape of the trilogy is, in important part, that of a progressive clearing of the atmosphere. At first we are in the dark. Utterances are oracular. Everything that happens, or that has happened already, is obscure and in need of working out. Gradually things become clearer. The death of Agamemnon, presented in symbolic forms by the utterances of Clytemnestra and Cassandra, is finally made plain. The Furies, who in *Agamemnon* are everywhere, their presence and activity constantly invoked, eventually appear: horrible indeed, but not, in the end, more than we can endure, and finding a niche in which their power will become positively valuable. The end of the trilogy resolves all the different questions, and reconciles gods and men.

Who Wears the Trousers in the House of Atreus?

Ruth Hazel

The question 'Who wears the trousers in the House of Atreus?' involves, of course, for those who know about dress in the ancient world, a pun. For the Greeks of fifth-century Athens, wearing trousers was a mark of non-Greekness; only barbarians – suspect Orientals – wore such degenerate and uncivilised leg garments (fragmentary visual evidence from vases shows trousers being worn by what look to be Persians). In modern understanding, to 'wear the trousers' in a household means to be The Man of the House, and the phrase is usually employed in a derogatory or critical sense when a woman is actually the one who seems to hold the reins of control, to dominate in an area she is not commonly expected to. The phrase signals a deviation from the norm.

Evidence of what we might describe as trousers being worn in fifth-century theatre is to be found on vases which show scenes from comedy; here, comic characters are shown wearing baggy Long Johns, to suggest a slave's bare legs or an old man's wrinkled skin. Vases featuring satyr play scenes also show the satyr actors in trousers, or rather, shaggy drawers with phallus appended to suggest the satyr's goat-form lower parts. To wear trousers, it seems, in Athenian theatre, was to signal some kind of otherness outside the norm of respectable Greek society; it would alert the audience to treat the trouser-wearing character with suspicion or laughter.

As the woman who, from the very first speech of the Watchman in *Agamemnon*, is described as having a man's brain in a woman's body, Clytemnestra must be a prime candidate for the title of 'the One Who Wears the Trousers in the House of Atreus'. It is she who occupies Agamemnon's palace while he is away fighting at Troy; she, with her lover, Aegisthus, occupies Agamemnon's bed. At line 259, the Chorusmen acknowledge Clytemnestra's power, but acknowledge, too, that she is only in that position of power because she represents her royal husband: 'For when the throne is empty of its man-lord, it is right and proper that we pay due honour to our ruler's wife', they circumspectly say. Metaphorically Clytemnestra is wearing Agamemnon's trousers, but she is entitled to, because that's what good wives do when their husbands are away. She boasts to the Herald that when Agamemnon returns he will find a wife:

> ... as faithful as she was the day he left, the obedient watch-dog of his house, the scourge of all that wish him ill, in all respects the same, her seal unbroken, even after all these years. I know no more of finding pleasure with another man or earning bad repute than I know how to plunge brute bronze into an icy bath to harden it.

If this had indeed been the case, Clytemnestra would have been a model wife – like Penelope, the chaste and faithful wife of Odysseus. However, as even the Watchman on the walls knows – and as the Elders of Argos certainly know – the Queen speaks with forked tongue. Only a naïve listener, or someone who, like the Herald, has been away from Argos for ten years, would take her declaration at face value, but the citizens of Argos who have, for ten years, been aware of the liaison between the queen and her husband's cousin, Aegisthus, have had no way of objecting to this scandal, which amounts almost to a pollution of the royal bed. The power which the queen lawfully wields as her husband's regent protects her both from any political rebellion and from overt personal criticism.

It has also to be said that Clytemnestra knows how to use 'woman's words', the deceptive and persuasive verbal power for which the mythic female women of Athenian drama were proverbially famous. She ends her speech describing the sack of Troy, as she imagines it, with the hope that the victorious Greeks will have a safe journey home – that they don't offend the gods by any desecration or blasphemy during the sack of the city. Even so, she says, for some 'the wrath and retribution of the dead' may be lying in wait … but these are 'a woman's words', she concludes, meaning, apparently, that women are always hoping for the best but fearful of the worst. The Chorus respond that her words have, in fact, been those of 'a rational and judicious man', which seems like a compliment, but may actually convey their mistrust of her. A woman who thinks and speaks like a man is an unnatural creature, someone of whom one should be deeply suspicious. Even more dangerous is a woman who apparently disclaims any pretensions to being as wise and powerful as a man.

Clytemnestra is never so dangerous as when she is playing the 'little woman', the devoted wife. (Directors of recent modern-dress productions have exploited this fact by having Clytemnestra reappear for the reception of Agamemnon dressed, not in a trouser suit or power-dressing shoulder-pads, but in a very feminine costume, as, for example, in Katie Mitchell's 1999 National Theatre production where Anastasia Hille wore a Fifties-style white and red full-skirted dress, and a blonde Eva Peron hairstyle.) Her seduction of Agamemnon (for that is what it is – an enticing of him to his deathbed) is a masterpiece of acting. She greets him with an effusive speech of welcome in which she first protests her continuing love for him and says how much she has missed him, describing her suicide attempts after false reports of his death had reached her; then she smoothly explains the absence of their child, and, lest Agamemnon might think she is still reproaching him for Iphigenia's death, hastily explains she is talking about Orestes. She hails Agamemnon as the only hope of his land; the watch-dog of the fold; the main beam or anchor of the ship of state; the chief pillar holding up the House of the country; dear as a beloved only son;

or an oasis to the parched; or first sight of land to sea-voyagers. He is entitled to such grandiose praise, she claims, and to make apparent his deserving, she has prepared a triumphal path of precious textile for him to tread as he enters his house. With this archetypal red carpet treatment, Clytemnestra, the Black Widow spider, invites the subject of her hatred and the object of her vengeance to walk into her parlour – or, rather, into the lustral bath which is to become his coffin. She not only strips him of his metaphorical trousers; she succeeds in persuading him to drop all his defences and encounter his death naked, unsuspecting, unarmed, but enmeshed in a net-like textile, the product of a woman's industry: only in this state will it be possible for the High King of Argos, head of the House of Atreus, to be defeated by a 'weak and feeble woman'.

Agamemnon had rightly been cautious in his response to Clytemnestra's words. He might well be unsure of his reception by his wife on his return to Argos since we can assume that, after the sacrifice of Iphigenia at Aulis, the couple would hardly have parted on the best of terms. In his wry reaction to her tour-de-force speech of welcome ('Clytemnestra, guardian of my house, your speech well matched my absence – both were much too long') Agamemnon addresses his wife as 'Daughter of Leda', which subtly reminds us that Clytemnestra is Helen's sister. Is Agamemnon wondering whether, with the reason she has for hating him, Clytemnestra might also prove untrustworthy to her husband? Certainly he baulks at behaving as, in her typically womanish excess, she invites him to. We cannot know whether his '... I'm not a pasha, either, so no genuflections, no salaams, no perorations ...' implies that the Clytemnestra actor actually did prostrate himself, as was customary for Persians to do before a royal person, but, if he did, it would certainly have been a powerful, and rather shocking, moment for the audience. Very properly, Agamemnon curtly rebukes Clytemnestra for treating him as if he were some kind of Persian despot; as far as he is concerned, her behaviour is worse than womanish; it is almost barbarian. She is treating him, he implies, as if he were the sort of person who would wear <u>trousers</u>!

From Clytemnestra's viewpoint, her husband <u>is</u> a kind of barbarian. He sacrificed his own daughter at Aulis in order to avert Artemis's displeasure and ensure the departure of the Greek fleet for Troy. The Chorus's first speech had given the normative view: Agamemnon was confronted with an impossible choice, and had 'clamped around his throat the leash of certainty'. As High King he had to make a decision, and his decision put his public role as leader of the Greek forces above his private role of father. However, the Chorus also comment that this privileging of political or public over personal bonds was made in a kind of mad fanaticism; although the sacrifice was carried out to appease a goddess, it was itself a sacrilege. The decision made by the king irrevocably set his fate, but it was also a kind of rite of passage for Agamemnon since, by making the choice he did, he ceased to be governed by social and affective bonds of marriage and fatherhood and became the leader of a war machine, implacable, dedicated, exempt from the normal rules of civilised conduct. In a modern sense of the word, he had become 'barbaric'.

When Agamemnon demurs at trampling Clytemnestra's triumphal textile, he does so, not simply because it seems to him an act of ostentation, a conspicuous and arrogant flaunting of wealth (rather like wiping the floor with a pashmina), but because it is also an act of self-aggrandizement amounting to hubris. Only the gods 'deserve such shows of adoration', he says:

> ... but for me, a man, to trample on such beautiful brocade brings only fear. I tell you: honour me – but as a man not as a god.

Wise man – perhaps too wise to be truly good, since his caution arises from fear of retribution for hubris, not from a wish to avoid committing hubris. In their stichomythic exchange, Clytemnestra tries a number of tacks to turn him to her will: would he do this if he had vowed to? what did he think his conquered counterpart, Priam, would have done? why be afraid of public opinion when the envy of others just shows how much you have achieved? In spite of the cumulative force of the logic of Agamemnon's answers to these questions, the clinching line in the argument seems to be Clytemnestra's asking him to allow her – silly, fanciful woman that she is – this one little victory over the great victor of Troy, to have her way on this one matter. 'If it's *your* will that you submit, yours is the victory truly', she says; a conqueror can afford to submit on such a minor point. By acting the woman and concealing her masculine will to wreak revenge, Clytemnestra achieves what force and logical argument could not. Agamemnon, in order to please her (or placate her? or simply in order to get inside the palace and into a nice hot bath?) acts out the role of a barbarian conqueror arrogantly trampling over the wealth of land and sea.

The fact that he believes that Priam might well have indulged in such triumphalist arrogance suggests that Agamemnon views the Trojans as a somewhat barbarian race. Although they share the same gods and the same ancestors as the Greeks, for the besieging army, the population of the seemingly impregnable city might well have seemed alien. The wealth of Troy the fallen city is inevitably counted in its women and its movable treasures. Agamemnon has brought back with him as slave concubine the princess-prophetess, Cassandra, the embodiment of the walled city, the virgin not even Apollo dared violate. She has become a trophy of Agamemnon's triumph. Aeschylus here prescribes a spectacular theatrical entry in having her brought on with Agamemnon, seated on a chariot piled high with war booty. The fact that, some forty years after the *Oresteia*, Euripides, in his *Electra* (c. 415 BCE), has Electra describe her mother as lolling around:

...lapped in the spoils of Troy, and Trojan
    waiting-maids
My father captured and brought home,
    stand[ing] by her throne,
Their Phrygian gowns buckled with golden
    clasps ...

            (tr. Vellacott, Penguin, pp.115-6)

– suggests that in Athenian drama the wealth of
Troy was indicative, at least when being enjoyed
by Greeks, of decadence. One might wonder
whether Aeschylus wanted his audience to view
Agamemnon, with his Trojan concubine, his
ostentatious display of loot and his acceptance of
an exotic triumphal progress across the orchestra
into the skene of the 'House of Atreus', as
someone whose manhood and Greekness had
been degraded and vitiated by contact with the
luxury and otherness of Troy.

Whoever is or is not wearing the trousers of
power in the House of Atreus, it certainly is not
Aegisthus. Even the Chorus of Elders, who
throughout the play stress their age and
impotence in the political disorder of Argos, call
him 'Woman!'. While Agamemnon went to fight,
they sneer at Aegisthus, he stayed at home and
seduced Clytemnestra. He was not even man
enough to wield the sword himself, but left the
actual murder to Clytemnestra. It is particularly
significant that Aeschylus made a major change
to the story of Agamemnon's murder as told in the
Odyssey. In Book Four, Menelaus tells
Telemachus how Aegisthus laid an ambush for

Agamemnon, and had him struck down while he sat at a banquet. (This account has a pleasing correspondence to the deceitful hospitality prepared by Agamemnon's father, Atreus, for Thyestes, Aegisthus's father.) A vase painting of c. 470 BCE also shows Aegisthus striking at Agamemnon with a sword and Clytemnestra apparently offering no more than vocal assistance. Aeschylus's Aegisthus makes a poor attempt at an excuse: 'to snare him was the woman's work', he says. When the Chorus demand why, having Agamemnon at his mercy, he didn't then kill him himself, Aegisthus blusters and threatens to silence these recalcitrant old men permanently. But the final word of authority is Clytemnestra's. She, in advising the Elders of Argos to make the best of things and disperse, accepting that justice has been done, claims to speak with 'woman's wisdom'. Again, she uses the cover of female diplomacy to effect a political manoeuvre: the quelling of potential rebellion by a show of power. Together, the man and the woman who have brought about their long wished-for revenges will govern in the House of Atreus. They will both wear the trousers.

And that concept – of joint rule by female and male, with the female conspicuously dominant – is in itself, for a fifth-century BCE Athenian audience, a kind of barbarism, an example of metaphoric trouser-wearing of another kind. The end of the *Agamemnon* is a truly unsettling one, and is a good example of the continuity which trilogies of this kind (in which all three plays

83

develop one narrative) would have had. The end is not closure but a pause for time to pass. We may therefore consider how the wearing of metaphorical trousers in this first part of the trilogy relates to the rest of the work.

In the final part of the *Oresteia*, Orestes is brought to trial before a jury of Athenians for the killing (whether murder or execution) of his mother, Clytemnestra. Apollo has acted as the defence attorney and the Furies as the prosecution, baying for blood and set on continuing forever the revenge ethic of which they are the functionaries. Earlier in the play, the Furies had argued with Apollo that the murder of a husband by his wife was less heinous than that of mother by son, since no blood connection exists between husband and wife, as is the case between parent and child. Apollo answered that this showed contempt for the bond of married love and disrespect to Zeus and Hera, the divine archetype of the married couple. It is at this point that Apollo decides to submit to the wisdom of Athene the intractable problem of whether Orestes is guilty of murder and deserves death. Athene gives her casting vote on the side of Orestes, agreeing with the argument that his obligation to revenge his male parent takes precedence over the bonds of affection, duty and respect which a son should pay to his mother. She throws her weight behind phallocentric authority:

No mother gave me birth. Therefore the

      father's claim
And male supremacy in all things, save to
      give
Myself in marriage, wins my whole heart's
      loyalty.
Therefore a woman's death, who killed her
      husband, is,
I judge, outweighed in grievousness by his.
                       (tr.Vellacott, p.172)

Athene seems to be saying that, since she had no mother and will never, herself, be a mother, she cannot really sympathise with the fate of Clytemnestra, and furthermore, that, because she retains her own independence by remaining unmastered by a husband, she can afford to acknowledge 'male supremacy in all things' as a general rule. To a modern audience, this seems outrageous; a selfish and sophistic attitude through which Athene awards herself the status of honorary male. Some critics see her, at this point, as corresponding to Clytemnestra, a woman with a male mind who takes control of the situation and dictates to the men around her what is or is not to happen. In Athens, Athene certainly wears the trousers.

However, whereas out of Clytemnestra's subversion of gender roles came murder, hatred, and the division of the House of Atreus (the unit of social community in *Agamemnon*), out of Athene's goddess-maleness comes reconciliation, a judicial system which deposes the revenge ethic, and benediction for the City of Athens.

If we consider the story of Agamemnon and Clytemnestra as distinct from the story of the House of Atreus (for that story we would need to go back, not one, but three generations, to Tantalus and his son, Pelops), we could see the final play in Aeschylus's *Oresteia* as, in one sense, completing the circle. The sacrifice of Iphigenia, for which Clytemnestra plans her revenge over the ten years of Agamemnon's absence, was demanded by another maiden-goddess: Artemis. As the Chorus of Elders of Argos recall, it was Artemis who held the Greek ships becalmed at Aulis because she was angry about the slaughter of innocent youth. What was that slaughter? Not, surely, the tearing apart of a pregnant hare by two eagles, the omen which the two brother-kings, Agamemnon and Menelaus, see as the Greek forces convene at Aulis. Calchas interprets the sign aright; the two royal birds <u>will</u> strike Troy and tear it apart. But he warns them that Artemis hates 'the eagles' feast', the slaughter of the innocent. It seems ironic, then, that she should demand as an offering from Agamemnon the slaughter of his innocent child. It is the slaughter of *Troy* she wants to prevent; if Agamemnon made the choice of a loving father, he would have had to disband the forces and give up the enterprise to which he had committed himself and all the Greeks: the recovery of Helen and the chastisement of Paris. He refused to lose face, credibility and authority in this way, and in doing what was, apparently, demanded by Artemis, committed a double offence in her eyes; first, the slaughter of innocent Iphigenia; then, pursuing his aim to destroy the city she favoured, Troy, and its innocents. So the story starts with a powerful maiden goddess demanding the killing of a child by its parent, and ends with another powerful maiden goddess exonerating a child for the killing of its parent. The moving deities for the start and close of the action of the *Oresteia* are female.

In some productions of the Agamemnon-Clytemnestra-Orestes story on the modern stage, directors have chosen to integrate that original intervention by a masterful female in the affairs of men by incorporating some, or all, of Euripides' *Iphigenia at Aulis* with Aeschylus's *Oresteia*. This was done by Ariane Mnouchkine in her version, *Les Atrides* (1990-2), where the focus of the whole play was on the figure of Clytemnestra. Showing Agamemnon's brutality and deception towards the women of his family goes some way to explaining, while not justifying, Clytemnestra's almost psychotic hatred for her husband. An earlier version by John Barton and Kenneth Cavander (*The Greeks*: RSC, 1979/80) was a trilogy made up from ten plays with extra material from Homer. It started with *Iphigenia at Aulis* and ended with *Iphigenia in Tauris*. This gave the end of the trilogy a Shakespearean Romance feel, with family reunion, a return from death by Iphigenia, whose apparent killing had started the whole cycle, and a generous acknowledgement and honouring of Artemis by her sister-goddess, Athene.

Overall, it would seem that in ancient Greek tragedy, trouser-wearing (in either of the two metaphorical senses I have identified) is not a happy experience. Certainly in the *Agamemnon* the subversive powerful female is explicitly condemned by the Chorus, who, although they are presented as 'old-womanish', are undoubtedly the normative voice. (In Katie Mitchell's NT production in 1999, the Chorus of the *Agamemnon* section was represented as disabled, wheel-chair-bound war veterans. In Purcarete's 1998 National Theatre of Craiova *Oresteia*, the Chorusmen had bald wigs, walking sticks and brief-cases, suggesting impotent bureaucrats.) But among the final defiant one-liners with which the Chorus leave the orchestra to the possession of the manly-woman and the womanish man is the statement that: 'Argive men will never grovel at the feet of a villain'. They are temporarily silenced, but exit still asserting the difference between the Greek man and the grovelling barbarian trouser-wearer.

There would undoubtedly have been many in the audience for the original performance of Aeschylus's *Oresteia* in 458BCE who had also witnessed his earlier play *Persians* (472BCE), the only extant Athenian tragedy on a subject of very recent history. In that play, Aeschylus had provided for his audience a spectacle of barbarian culture, with Persian costumes and movement. The *Agamemnon*, with its references to oriental luxury and decadence and its foregrounding of a female character, may well have recalled for its audience that earlier celebration of the victory of Greek over barbarian.

[Quotations from the *Agamemnon* are from David Stuttard's translation; quotations from the *Eumenides* and Euripides' *Electra* are from Philip Vellacott's translations for the Penguin editions.]

The Dramatic Technique of *Agamemnon*

David Raeburn

Agamemnon was composed when European drama was in its infancy, but it is one of the most perfectly made and powerful plays ever written. How does it *work* as a drama? That is to say, how does it succeed in engaging and holding our rapt attention?

On the face of it, the play is an extraordinarily static affair. In a physical sense, very little indeed seems to *happen*. The subject matter in plot terms is the return of Agamemnon from the siege of Troy and the murder of the king by his wife Clytemnestra and her lover Aegisthus. When the piece is performed in the original Greek, it takes a good hour of stage time before Agamemnon actually enters, and we are kept waiting about another forty minutes before we hear his death-cries offstage. We never see Clytemnestra overtly machinating or plotting with Aegisthus. Their adulterous relationship is only darkly hinted at and Aegisthus is not even referred to by name until the murder is over. What sense are we to make of this, and how can we possibly find it exciting and dramatic?

To find an answer to this question, we need to consider the kind of drama which Aeschylus was writing for competitive performance before the body of Athenian citizens at a religious festival in a large open-air theatre. We know that tragedy began about seventy years before the first production of the *Orestean Trilogy* (of which *Agamemnon* is Act I) and that the earliest examples of this new art-form were played by a single actor, who was probably the poet himself, and a Chorus. The poet was assuming a role similar to that of the rhapsodes or professional reciters of the Homeric poems who would have impersonated the different characters of the epic as well as telling the story in the voice of a narrator. The Chorus derived from a different genre altogether: hymns sung and danced to the accompaniment of the lyre on ritual occasions in honour of gods or heroes. These hymns had a definite *purpose*, which was to please the god or hero concerned and so to ensure the prosperity of the local community in such things as the growth of the crops or the fertility of the women. The sung words were felt to have a magical, spell-binding power which would produce the desired result; but they had to be the *right* words which the gods would find pleasing and so guarantee a favourable outcome. The *wrong* words would be ill-omened and affect the issue adversely. There is no doubt that a belief in the power of words to affect the future was deeply ingrained among the Greeks of Aeschylus' time. Even we retain some traces of this in our won secular age: we wish people luck and say "Bless you!"; we have a gut feeling that it is unlucky to boast or make extravagant predictions; we are uneasy when people make gloomy prophecies, as though this increases the chances of our fears being realised.

Given Greek tragedy's beginnings, let us see where tragedy had got to with Aeschylus, the first of the great three tragedians whose work we have inherited. We know from Aristotle that he introduced a second actor who could engage in dialogue with the first actor as well as the Chorus, and that Sophocles added a third who was already employed by 458 B.C. when the *Oresteia* was originally performed. What is interesting, though, is that although *Agamemnon* requires three actors to play all the parts, the *bulk* of the play is still composed for Chorus with one soloist onstage. There is only one piece of *stichomythia* (line-for-line dialogue) when two of the actors are in formal conversation with one another and this passage (when Clytemnestra persuades Agamemnon to walk into his palace over purple garments) is all the more striking for its uniqueness.

When it comes to the Chorus in *Agamemnon*, it is even more important to think of tragedy's start. Not only does the Chorus play the leading role in the drama, but their original ritual function is retained *in the context of the play's action*. There are two places in the *Oresteia* where the power of words is exploited very obviously. One is the great formal invocation in the second play, *Libation Bearers*, when Orestes and Electra along with the Chorus call on the spirit of Agamemnon to rise from the grave and assist them in the terrible task of matricidal revenge. The second is the Binding Song which the Furies chant over the fugitive Orestes in *Eumenides* after they have caught up with him in Athens, the effect of which is only averted by the arrival of Athena in response to a prayer by Orestes. However, the power of ritually used language does not simply apply to overtly ritualistic acts. It is operative *throughout* the choral songs in *Agamemnon*. The Argive Elders' words are vested with a magical power to affect the issues of Agamemnon's return from Troy and impending murder either propitiously or adversely. What happens in their songs is that they keep trying to say the helpful, well-omened thing; but their train of thought and utterance constantly leads them to say what is ill-omened and therefore practically damaging to Agamemnon's interest. This way we can see the long choral movements not as tedious interludes for poetic reminiscence or platitudinous moralising but as *events* no less than the 'episodes' which feature the solo characters and (in one scene) two characters in conflict. Indeed the *fundamental* conflict in the play, considered technically, is that between words of good omen for Agamemnon and words of bad omen.

Furthermore, if we accept that the principle of *euphemia*, right utterance, applies as much to what the solo actors say as it does to the Chorus, then a great deal that we may find puzzling starts to become much clearer. In particular, it explains why the long build-up to Agamemnon's entrance is so impressively absorbing, despite the absence of action in any practical sense. In the first part of the play, those who are on Agamemnon's side – that is, the Chorus, the Watchman and the Herald – keep trying, though failing, to use propitious language; while Clytemnestra, whose intentions are hostile to the king, is doing the reverse while *pretending* to be benevolent. The result of this extended interplay of words is that when the great conqueror of Troy proudly enters in his chariot, we are *overwhelmingly* sure that he is doomed.

Before I substantiate this further, I must say something very briefly about Aeschylus' Trilogy as a whole, as this has a bearing on much of the detail to be explored. *Agamemnon* states a problem which is brought to a head in the second play and finally resolved in the third. Although the *Oresteia* has many interesting themes, the essential issue is that of retributive justice based on revenge. The law of retaliation implicit in the blood-feud or family vendetta is shown to be tragically futile because it entails an endless chain of crime and punishment. It is important to see Agamemnon's murder an as item in a series. It has its antecedents in the sacrifice of Iphigenia (who represents the many innocent Greeks and Trojans destroyed in the war), the rape of Helen and the sins of Agamemnon's father Atreus for which the son is being punished. It has its horrific sequel in the predicament of Agamemnon's son Orestes who is compelled as an act of *duty* to commit the appalling *crime* of killing his mother. The vicious chain is only broken in a new social and judicial context, when Orestes is tried before an Athenian court and the city-state takes responsibility for his punishment or acquittal. In this sense the *Oresteia* can be seen as a kind of parable about man's development in society. That is why the past and the future play such an important part in the ritual sequence which constitutes *Agamemnon*. Now to the play itself.

Prologue (lines 1-39)

Note that the Watchman begins with a prayer to the gods to 'end my suffering'. The character, of course, is thinking of an end to his weary watching on the roof of the House of Atreus. He is looking forward to the appearance of the beacon signal which will announce the capture of Troy. But the same Greek words are used by Apollo in the third play to prophesy Orestes' final acquittal by the court at Athens. They can thus be seen as an image of the 'end of suffering' implicit in the resolution of the blood-feud in the context of the Athenian *polis*.

Before long the Watchman introduces a theme which established an often repeated pattern. When he tries to remedy his sleeplessness (and cheer himself up) by singing or whistling, he says he falls to weeping for the misfortunes of the house. This is just what happens at once. He sights the fire of the beacon with great joy and calls on Agamemnon's wife to raise 'the women's cry of *good omen*'. But within a few lines his joy had been overcast by a cloud of foreboding

95

regarding his master's return. He will not give utterance to his fears, though. 'This house, this building, if it could but speak, would say it all most clearly' – and that is all he is prepared to give away. (The audience knows he is referring to Clytemnestra's adultery with Aegisthus during Agamemnon's absence.) To go any further than these cryptic words would be ill-omened.

Parodos (lines 40-257)

The pattern of confident utterance, soon to be overshadowed by fear, is repeated several times in the long ritual sequence of the choral entrance-song. It begins with a powerful picture of the two sons of Atreus, Menelaus and Agamemnon, sent by Zeus as a Fury (Avenging Spirit) on Troy; but this soon yields to the Argive Elders' expression of their own weakness and powerlessness. In the next section, the excitement and hope generated by Clytemnestra's fires on the altars round Argos is tempered by insatiable, heart-consuming anxiety. A fresh start is made when the metre changes from the introductory anapaests to rolling dactyls and the Chorus recounts the omen which sent the Greek expedition on its way, the omen of the two eagles (the two kings) tearing the pregnant hare (Troy and her innocent young). But this apparently positive utterance has negative connotations, as revealed in the omen's interpretation by the prophet Calchas: the goddess Artemis, as patroness of young animals, 'is sickened by the eagles' feast', and her hatred may conjure up the contrary winds at Aulis which presage a 'sacrifice barbaric' (of Iphigenia) and, waiting behind, 'the child-avenging Fury which will not forget.' A refrain rings out three times during this part of the song. "Sorrow, sing sorrow, but let the good prevail!" This is a song of sorrow. All we can do is to cry "Good!" in the hope that all will in the end be well.

At this point the dactyls abruptly change to solemn trochees, as the chorus invokes the name of Zeus, who instituted the rule for mankind of 'learning through suffering' – which I take to be a positive doctrine of hope, implying that 'from suffering comes understanding'. If that is right, the Elders are attempting at this point of their ritual to avert the veil effect of their previous words by calling on Zeus, who can enable them to 'exorcise the dull ache of foreboding'. The prayer is linked metrically with Agamemnon's predicament at Aulis before the metre changes once again to the taut 'syncopated iambic' rhythm which recurs throughout the Trilogy in connection with the tragic motif of sin and retribution. The Chorus goes on to describe the storm which delayed the greek ships, the king's terrible moral dilemma and his eventual decision to sacrifice his daughter Iphigenia. The doctrine of 'learning through suffering' is hard to understand if it is applied to Agamemnon personally, since *he* clearly learns nothing as the play progresses. However, the passage makes real sense in the context of the Trilogy as a whole. *Mortals* achieve understanding when the futility of the blood-feud reaches such a horrendous point (as it does when a man can kill his own mother as an act of *justice*), that humanity learns from its suffering and finds a way through the judicial system represented by the Athenian *polis*. The Hymn to Zeus is thus a crucial act in the ritual performance of the *Oresteia*. Its efficacy as an invocation is not immediately proved, but it works in the end. In the first two plays, the good does *not* prevail, only sorrow; but in the third it does.

The narrative of Iphigenia's sacrifice rises to its climax. The innocent girl is lifted over the altar, gagged to muffle her ill-omened cries, glancing pitifully at her sacrificers. But the Elders stop short before the fatal stroke. 'The rest I neither saw nor tell of, but the crafts of Calchas *were not unfulfilled*. It is true that Justice assigns understanding to those who have suffered, but as to the coming issue – you will hear it when it happens. Till then farewell to it.' The Elders are trying desperately hard to avoid saying *outright* that Agamemnon must eventually pay for the killing of his daughter with his own blood. Reticence, euphemism is the order of the play.

First Episode (lines 258-354)

The following scene in which we see the Chorus with Clytemnestra is extremely peculiar by any normal standards of dramaturgy. Let me attempt a summary: 'Enter Clyt., who confidently announces the capture of Troy last night. "How can you possibly know?" asks the Cho. in amazement. Long speech in reply from Clyt. who

98

describes the chain of beacons which have relayed the news in a string of place-names extending from Troy to Mycenae. At the end the Leader says he would like to hear the speech over again, from start to finish. Second long speech from Clyt., but on different lines altogether. She offers a detailed picture of the scene in Troy on the night after the capture and issues a warning: the Greeks must not destroy the Trojan shrines, as they still have to return home and much may yet go wrong for them. The Leader then says he is now convinced that the news is true and prepares to give thanks to the gods. Exit Clyt.'

What has *happened* in this very strange scene? We have encountered the awesome figure of Clytemnestra, but the plot has not been advanced a whit. What is the queen *doing*? Consider her opening two lines, words apparently of good omen: 'With good news, as the proverb says, may dawn spring from her mother night.' But the Greek words for 'her mother night' have a sinister resonance as they also suggest a 'kindly mother', that is a mother who might avenge an injured child. Take the Beacon Speech next, an excitingly vivid piece of dramatic poetry in which Clytemnestra seems to have the fire god Hephaestus under her personal control. It can be seen as symbolic, with the queen beckoning on and hailing the fire of destruction, the vengeance of Zeus which struck down guilty Tory, as it comes bounding and blazing over the sea to strike the palace of Agamemnon. I believe myself that we can go further than that. If one looks at the place-names, they can all be shown to have sinister associations with feminine treachery, the death of kings, ambushes and the like – even the made-up names which cannot be found on the map. Under a cloak of innocence, Clytemnestra is using ill-omened words, like a witch, to damage the object of her vengeful hatred, her husband Agamemnon. The Beacon Speech is not just a lively description but an aggressive *action*: she is covertly driving verbal nails into Agamemnon's coffin, sticking pins into his wax image. This explains the Leader's puzzling reaction that he would like to hear it all through again. There are indeed layers of ambiguity and ulterior significance which could not be easily grasped at a first hearing.

Clytemnestra's second speech, giving the scene in Troy after the capture (very convincingly, though how could she know *this* time?), is sinister in a more obvious way. She mentions the sad plight of the Trojans but also speaks of disarray in the Greek army; and then she goes on to rehearse all the dangers in the Greek situation, so as to make them the more likely to happen: offence to the gods, reawakening the suffering of the dead and (for good measure) *accidental* disasters. There is a menacing defiance in Clytemnestra's exit lines.

To sum up, this odd episode makes sense as action, as drama, if we realise that the language is used in a 'ritualistic' way, for the purpose of blessing or cursing, and reckoned as such to be actually helpful or damaging to Agamemnon.

1st Stasimon (lines 355-474, with coda 475-87)

The second long choral ode is another wonderful movement. Its content is complex, but the essential point to grasp from a dramatic angle is that it begins with a well-omened paean of thanksgiving to Zeus for the victory over Troy and ends with an ill-omened denunciation of the sons of Atreus. The son follows a train of associated ideas in which the laws which governed Paris' crime (in abducting Helen) and Paris' punishment are seen also to apply to Agamemnon. The subject matter and imagery shift as the Chorus 'tracks out' the chain of cause and effect. However, the syncopated iambic rhythm and the metrical structure remain constant as though to underline the principle – the inexorable law of sin and retribution – which gives this song its unity and logic.

Note the devastating conclusion: 'I prefer unenvied prosperity. May I never be a *sacker* of *cities*' – another huge nail in Agamemnon's coffin. Then in a curious appendage, the Elders back-track and start to wonder whether the beacon messages were reliable after all – astonishingly, in the light of their earlier assent. This is intelligible, though, if we remember that their acceptance of the beacon news motivated the triumphant start of their ritual song, which has led them inexorably to a dismal conclusion that they would now prefer to unsay.

2nd Episode (lines 489-680)

The Herald scene is likewise a movement from well-omened to ill-omened utterance. From the plot angle, it tells us nothing more than that Agamemnon is on his way; but the episode is devastating in its dramatic effect. The Herald is given three marvellous speeches. The first, in which he movingly greets his native soil after his nine-year absence and proclaims Agamemnon's triumph, can be seen as almost entirely propitious – except when he innocently blurts out that the Trojan sanctuaries of the gods have been obliterated by the Greeks (we remember Clytemnestra's warning and shudder). In his second speech the Herald continues with a graphic description of all the horrors which the Greek soldiers have had to experience at war. But all that is over now, he says; the good outweighs the bad.

Reenter Clytemnestra, and the atmosphere at once clouds over. She frustrates the Herald's mission by telling him she knew all the time that her husband was coming. Her message of greeting to Agamemnon is chilling in its malevolent ambiguity. 'I know no more of finding pleasure with another man', she says, 'than I know how to plunge brute bronze into an icy bath to harden it' – and we immediately think of the bronze sword which she will later 'plunge' in Agamemnon's blood when his body lies in the bath.   Exit Clytemnestra again, and now the propitious mood is lost for ever.

'How about Menelaus?' asks the Leader, and that tears it. The Herald protests, 'It is not fitting to pollute a *day of good omen with tongue of bad news*', as he proceeds in his final speech to describe the terrible storm, betokening the gods' anger against the Greeks, which has destroyed the fleet and left only Agamemnon with a few survivors. The Herald leaves the stage shattered, like the ships he has described.

2nd Stasimon (lines 681-761)

The next choral song brings us to the final stage in the ritual which culminates in Agamemnon's appearance in person. The ode is complex this time in its metre as well as its thought. It begins with the recollection of Helen: she was rightly named (*'Hell* in ships and *hell* in men and *hell* in cities'). Names are omens being translated into realities, words becoming facts. The ideas about the punishment of the sinner which the Elders have enunciated in their previous song are shortly to come alive in visible action onstage. Helen, the Chorus continues, affected the Trojans like a lion-cub which is cheerfully reared as a pet in a household but later shows its true nature and creates a shambles – good displaced by evil once more.

The spell is wound tighter as the Chorus reflects that prosperity conjoined with sin brings disaster.

From now on we think less of Troy and more of Agamemnon. The iambic rhythm returns and grows more insistent. '*Hubris* (sinful pride) breeds *hubris* ... Justice abandons a house that is wealthy but sinful ... she guides all to its *appointed end.*'

Enter Agamemnon, the prosperous sinner, in his chariot to *his* appointed end. The charm's wound up. The Chorus hails him, 'Come, my king, offspring of Atreus, *city-sacker* of Troy!' No man in drama is so surely doomed before he has spoken a single word.

I hope that enough has already been said to illustrate the importance and power of 'magic words' rather than physical actions as the chief basis of Aeschylus' dramatic technique. Careful study of the play's text and logic reveals that the first hour of *Agamemnon* is not a dull, static affair but potentially an intensely exciting and dynamic experience. Space allows me to pick out only two details in the latter part of the play by way of conclusion.

After Agamemnon has been lured by Clytemnestra into the palace over purple garments and we now await his death-cries, the drama is held in suspended animation in an amazing scene when the prophetess Cassandra, whom Agamemnon has brought home as his concubine, unites the whole series of past, present and future crimes in her frenzied visions. At one point she speaks of a wife murdering her husband in the bath and later of the secret destruction planned for her master (Agamemnon) by the detestable tongue of a bitch (Clytemnestra). But because of the curse laid on Cassandra by Apollo that no one would ever believe her prophecies, the Chorus is completely mystified by her cryptic utterances. 'I tell you: you will look on *Agamemnon dead*,' bursts out Cassandra. The Leader's appalled reaction is 'No malediction, wretched woman! Hush what you're saying now.' She has spoken the dreadful words which the Elders have been trying throughout the play's ritual sequence *not* to say.

Secondly, when Agamemnon is finally murdered and his death-cries ring out offstage, Aeschylus achieves the most extraordinary effect. He shatters the corporate personality of his Chorus and splits it up into its component parts. Instead of a united body, performing an orderly and dignified ritual, we watch twelve crusty individual old men, arguing in shapeless confusion about what ought to be done. It is as though a bomb were to be dropped on a cathedral at the most solemn moment of a great religious event like a coronation. Some have found this a ridiculous scene. But Aeschylus could not have hit on a more imaginative stroke to express the tragic dissonance which the death of Agamemnon, king and husband, at the hands of his own wife signifies in the scheme of his great Trilogy.

Agamemnon Solo

Lorna Hardwick

Nowadays, *Agamemnon* seems to be performed on its own nearly as frequently as it is in Aeschylus' trilogy *The Oresteia*. In the last few years it has been performed by **aod** (Actors of Dionysus) in 1999, in 2000 by the NewVic as Triche Keyhoe's version *Children of Clytemnestra*, by students in Newcastle in Tony Harrison's translation and in Athens by the Theseion Theatre as *The Ghost Sonata*. Staging the play on its own inevitably places more stress on the situation of the name figure and the Athens production, directed by Michael Marmarinos, represented Agamemnon as an English-speaking stranger to his own land of Greece.

When the complete trilogy is staged this tends to be in the repertoire of the larger companies, often with international tours. After the iconic productions of the 1980s (which included the Royal Shakespeare Company's *The Greeks* in 1980, Peter Stein's 1980 Berlin production revived in 1994 and also staged in Greece and Russia, Karolos Koun's Theatro Technis productions in Greece in 1980 and 1982, Peter Hall's National Theatre production in Harrison's translation in 1981) more followed in the 1990s. Le Theatre du Soleil toured with *Les Atrides*, directed by Ariane Mnouchkine, in 1992. The Craiova Theatre Company of Romania, directed by Silviu Purcarete toured Europe in 1998 and the following year the Royal National Theatre staged Ted Hughes' version, directed by Katie Mitchell (in this production, *Agamemnon* was renamed *The Home Guard* and took up half the performance).

Agamemnon is certainly a substantial play in its own right. At 1,673 lines it is Aeschylus' longest play of those that survive (the second play in the trilogy, *The Libation Bearers* has 1, 076 lines and the final play, *The Eumenides*, has 1,047 lines). However, it is not only its greater length which makes it so powerful and so suitable for performance on its own. Its range of imagery and allusion is also considerable. It is in this play that the events surrounding Agamemnon's return from Troy are broadened from conflict within the family to embrace social, political and religious dimensions. Aeschylus' treatment of Agamemnon's return and death included significant adaptations from material in Homer and the Epic Cycle. The most important change is that it is Clytemnestra and not Aegisthus who is the prime mover in the killing of Agamemnon.

The characters in Aeschylus include those of lesser social status (the Watchman, the Chorus of Old Men, the Herald) who are nevertheless important as narrators, commentators, interpreters and sources of religious insight. They contribute to the establishment of the trilogy's themes of revenge and power struggle. Theatrically, the play offers tremendous staging opportunities. It is set in front of the palace where the killing is to take place but a sense of wider application is established by the position of the Watchman high on the roof, searching the sky for the flaming beacon which will signal victory for the Greeks at Troy. The figure of Cassandra, the Trojan captive who is princess and prophetess as well as victim, expresses not only the suffering which accompanies war but also the continuing complexities in the relationship between Greek and non-Greek after Troy. There are gripping theatrical moments - the confrontation between Agamemnon and Clytemnestra, her successful tempting of her husband to enter the house by walking over the spectacular carpet, Cassandra's eventual intervention after 300 lines of silence and the revealing of the dead bodies and the net with which Agamemnon was ensnared in his bath.

My interest in this article is in the effects of staging the play on its own, including the ways in which the relationships between the central characters are shaped by the more limited confines of the single play. It is clear from the examples of performance that I have given above that solo staging is more likely to be by a smaller or touring company. This has practical effects on the production values because of the likelihood that the acting space will be smaller than that of the commercial theatre (and also variable from venue to venue); scenery may have to be easily transportable and lighting design and stage effects simpler. The budget will certainly be more limited and together with the smaller acting space this limits the numbers in the Chorus and thus shapes the nature of its movement and choreography. There is also less potential for having specially composed live music. The composition of the audience (or, rather, the assumptions made about it) are also likely to be more variable with smaller and touring productions. Apart from regional variation, the audience may also be unpredictable in its degree of knowledge about ancient drama (some will be studying or teaching the play but others may experience Greek drama for the first time). The audience may vary in age and social background (in contrast to the more restricted middle-aged middle-class stereotypes now associated with commercial theatre) and it will almost certainly vary in its assumptions about Greek drama and in the socio-cultural hinterland of expectations and experiences brought to the theatre.

These practical considerations in solo staging thus interact with the effects from within. Detached from the trilogy, certain aspects inevitably become less prominent – for example, the continuation of the revenge cycle through Orestes' killing of Clytemnestra in *The Libation Bearers* and the resulting pollution as well as the socio-political aspects of the eventual conflict resolution, especially the move to a new order of justice and the role of Athena in bringing this about in *The Eumenides*. In contrast, the relationship between Clytemnestra and Agamemnon as individuals and their respective responsibilities for what happens looms larger.

The question of justice becomes more personal (and so potentially more anachronistic in the way that it is communicated). As a result, the staging of certain aspects of the play becomes crucial in ensuring the coherence of the play within its own terms and in shaping the audience's response (especially when the audience is unlikely to have detailed knowledge of the rest of the trilogy). Two of these aspects are particularly important and I propose to discuss each in turn with the aim of bringing out some of the choices open to the translator/script writer, the director and, indirectly, the audience and in suggesting ways in which they are interrelated. The two are: Agamemnon's sacrifice of Iphigenia and the Carpet or Tapestry scene. The discussion will compare the ways in which they are handled when the play was performed alone and when it was staged as a major part of the trilogy.

Agamemnon's sacrifice of Iphigenia

Of course this sacrifice does not actually take place within *Agamemnon* but is narrated in a key section of the substantial opening Chorus (the whole Chorus is over 220 lines). How it is handled is therefore crucial in developing relationships within the play and in shaping the audience's perceptions of Agamemnon long before he appears on the stage. How this sequence is played establishes the attitude of the Chorus and the audience to the moral and psychological status of Agamemnon and Clytemnestra. It may arouse sympathy for Agamemnon. It may establish a rationale for Clytemnestra to desire revenge on Agamemnon. Exceptionally, it may do both.

The part of the Chorus most closely associated with the sacrifice of Iphigenia runs from lines 184-257 in Aeschylus but it also relates closely to the images introduced from line 104, in which the exploits of Agamemnon and his brother Menelaus are likened to those of eagles swooping on a hare and tearing it apart to feast on its unborn young. The Chorus reports that Calchas, the seer attached to the Greek army, is fearful that this may arouse the anger of the goddess Artemis, protector of wildlife. The Chorus is conscious of the power of its role as narrator –

Authority and knowledge. I have the knowledge, the authority to tell the journey's omen

(Stuttard, 1999, 2)

At this point, Clytemnestra does not speak but she has been directly addressed by the Chorus so we must assume that she, like the audience, is the focus of the Chorus' narrative. The Chorus goes on to describe how the Greek fleet was assailed by storms at Aulis, how the army became discontented and how Calchas decreed that Artemis would only be placated if Agamemnon sacrificed his young daughter, Iphigenia. Agamemnon's choice is presented by the Chorus as being between two horrors – deserting the army or polluting his hands by killing his daughter, 'Each way lies horror. How can I jump ship and fail my allies? No. In her fury, supernatural, untamed, the goddess lusts for sacrifice of virgin blood to stay the storm – and that is right and proper' (Stuttard, 1999, 4).

The Chorus then describes the prelude to the sacrifice, the gagging of Iphigenia. She is held 'firm above the altar, like an animal, face-down, all wrapped close in the fabric of her robes...her yellow robes, dyed deep in purest saffron, fell heavy to the ground... Calchas' visions come to pass' (Stuttard, 1999, 4).

Critics love to dissect Agamemnon's dilemma but this inevitably involves psychological anachronism. However, their concern with the choices open to Agamemnon does anticipate the temptation for a modern audience to make judgements about his actions. In Aeschylus, the Chorus attaches no specific blame to Agamemnon but Stuttard's translation conveys an implicit comment on the underlying cultural inevitability - 'Fanaticism gives men strength...it goads men on to cruelty and guides their path to ruin. So he submitted. He became the priest of sacrifice and offered his own daughter as a bulwark in a war of vengeance for a woman's sake, first rite of passage for the fleet' (Stuttard, 1999, 4). The Chorus' account of the situation aligns the sacrifice with 'a war of vengeance'. The overt reference is to Troy but there is an ironic hint at the possibility of future vengeance against Agamemnon. In her speech to the

Chorus after Agamemnon has been killed, Clytemnestra picks up both the image and the complicity of the Chorus –

> O but you showed no opposition to my husband when he broke our faith, when – like it was a sheep he killed, picked for its fleece from all the flocks we own – he sacrificed his daughter, my baby I loved more than anything, a lullaby to soothe the winds from Thrace. Should you not have exiled *him* in retribution for unleashing such pollution?
>
> (Stuttard, 1999, 27).

When the play is performed alone, the details of the staging of the Chorus' narrative of the sacrifice of Iphigenia assume particular importance in defining the relationship between Agamemnon and Clytemnestra. In the text of the play, the Chorus does not take sides; it reports what happened, including the words of Calchas. In the **aod** production of 1999, the sacrifice was represented on the stage in a mime in which Iphigenia struggled to escape from the disabling bonds of the saffron robe. The Chorus members took on new identities (Agamemnon, Calchas, Iphigenia – even Clytemnestra's presence was suggested) in order to enact the sacrifice, with one Chorus member retaining a narrative role.

In the RNT production of the trilogy in the same year, Iphigenia also appeared on stage gagged, but then moved away, separated from the other actors and the audience by sitting on a balcony above the stage. A video image of her face was projected on to the doors of the palace and she became a constant ghostly presence. This picked up visually the effect of Ted Hughes' text, in which the words of the Chorus moved away from Aeschylus and explored Agamemnon's dilemma as an internal monologue (with his voice recorded on tape). The Chorus described the sacrifice as if it were happening in the present, emphasising the brutality and thus the betrayal by her father in an almost voyeuristic passage ('Pity is like a butterfly in a fist/As the knuckles whiten', Hughes, 1999, 16).

This prominence given to the sacrifice of Iphigenia is a feature of many modern productions (Mnouchkine's *Les Atrides* even preceded the Oresteia trilogy with Euripides' *Iphigenia at Aulis*). The effect is compounded when Agamemnon is staged alone since the sacrifice establishes the role of Agamemnon as polluter and provides a rationale for the prominence of Clytemnestra's role in his murder. If the whole trilogy is performed there is more room for exploring the nuances of Agamemnon's situation. In either case, the way in which the sacrifice is staged shapes the audience's attitude towards the main characters and may create a counterbalance with a contemporary audience's imaginative sympathy towards Agamemnon as a traumatised returner from a long and debilitating war. It may also mitigate hostility to Clytemnestra's adultery and active role in the murder.

The Carpet Scene

Although the play bears his name, Agamemnon does not appear until line 782 when the play is almost half over and he speaks only 84 lines in total (in contrast to the 128 lines of the Herald and the 64 lines allocated to Aegisthus for his minor role). When he returns, Agamemnon is accompanied by Cassandra, daughter of Priam, who has been allocated to him by the army as his concubine as part of the spoils of war. Like Iphigenia she is a symbol of pollution as her rapes by the Greeks violate the sanctity of her designation as Apollo's priestess. (There is also some transposition of imagery between the two in the sense that Clytemnestra refers to Cassandra as needing 'to bear the bridle easily before she lets her life's blood bubble from her', Stuttard, 1999, 18.) The production choices made in respect of her costume, movement, gestures and speech shape the audience's perceptions of her as princess, priestess, barbarian, victim of rape – or whore, which is how she is categorised by Clytemnestra. In the 1999 production by **aod**, the Chorus greeted Agamemnon's entry with 'locker-room' chants, which ceased only when quelled by the entrance of Clytemnestra. Agamemnon's behaviour towards Cassandra also denied her fully human status. Dressed in a Nazi-style black leather coat, he dragged her on a long chain. On all fours, she cowered behind a pillar, hissing and spitting at the Chorus as they taunted her.

After a tense exchange, Clytemnestra entices

Agamemnon to enter the palace by walking over a red carpet formed by expensive dyed tapestries. Some critics have interpreted Agamemnon's actions as an exercise in conspicuous consumption but there are also wider implications, suggesting that Agamemnon's surrender to overweening pride shows how he regards every inheritance as at his own disposal – whether human or material, whether in his own house or in the wider world. At this point the language in Hughes' version recalls Iphigenia – 'This heaped-up spilled-out wealth of my own house./ Do I make too much of it?' (Hughes, 1999, 46). As with the sacrifice of Iphigenia, he overcomes his own scruples – in this case a fear of appearing like an eastern potentate and accepting honours which should be reserved for the gods. David Stuttard's 1999 translation communicated these elements by making Agamemnon describe the tapestries in religious terms – 'These are not carpets, no, but sacred chasubles [fabrics used for vestments in Christian rituals]... I feel contrition so to trample on this house's wealth, to waste our riches...so this is how I come home – treading grape-red tapestries, a path of blood' (Stuttard, 1999, 15-17).

The visual representation of this last element was dominant in the staging of the carpet scene in the RNT Hughes/Mitchell version. Agamemnon was not only entering the palace to meet his own death, but in so doing he trod on a 'carpet' made up from the red (blood soaked) dresses of small children (similar to the dress of Iphigenia). The programme to the production included photographs showing children's clothes, shoes and toys labelled like exhibits in a criminal trial. Iphigenia goose-stepped after her father as he trod the path to the palace, then leapt onto his shoulders for a 'piggy-back'. During Clytemnestra's speech defending and celebrating her actions, Iphigenia reappeared and climbed into the bath containing the bodies of Agamemnon and Cassandra, nestling up to her father. This was perhaps a visual representation of Clytemnestra's claim that there would be no mourning for Agamemnon in the house but that it would be Iphigenia who would await Agamemnon in the underworld ('sublime reunion beside the racing streams of death' in Stuttard's translation, 1999, 29).

The sacrifice of Iphigenia and Agamemnon's entry to the palace and to his death are key dramatic moments in the play. In Aeschylus the first is narrated, the second enacted but they are linked in the internal imagery of the play as well as in the wider themes of the trilogy. When *Agamemnon* is performed alone there is an increased focus on the name character and on the dynamics of his relationship with Clytemnestra. In both solo and trilogy productions the communication of this relationship is shaped by the decisions of the translator/scriptwriter, the director and designer. In Stuttard's 1999 translation Clytemnestra has the last word – 'And what he did, the same was done to him in equal measure. So now he can no longer boast, now death has come now retribution has been paid in full for his transgressions' (Stuttard, 1999, 28). She regards her actions as having closed the circle of revenge. Only among the final lines of the Chorus is there a presage of what is to come – 'if the spirit of revenge should bring Orestes home' (Stuttard, 1999, 31). In bringing out the implications for the cycle of revenge of the sacrifice of Iphigenia, solo productions of the play can anticipate the themes of the rest of the trilogy as well as heightening for modern audiences the psychological complexities of the relationship between Agamemnon and Clytemnestra.

References

Ted Hughes, *Aeschylus: The Oresteia, a New Version*, London, Faber and Faber, 1999

David Stuttard (tr.) *Agamemnon*, Actors of Dionysus, York, 1999

(Since neither of these publications includes line numbers, all references are to the relevant pages.)

aod publications

Further collections of essays on the following plays are also available:

Aeschylus   *Agamemnon*
                 Choephoroi

Sophocles   *Ajax*
                 Antigone
                 Oedipus the King

Euripides   *Bacchae*
                 Electra
                 Hippolytus
                 Medea
                 Trojan Women

For information about any of these, as well as translations, audiobooks and videos, please contact

actors of dionysus,
44-46 old steine, brighton, uk bn1 1nh

t +0044 1273 320 396 • f +0044 1273 220 025
e info@actorsofdionysus.com